Unearthing Nature's Secrets

Dr. Jurgen Klein

Copyright © 2009 by Jurgen Klein

Published by: Dr. Jurgen and Karin Klein
JK Investment Trust
The Sullivan Estate & JK7 SPA Retreat
59-338 Wilinau Rd.
Haleiwa, HI 96712, U.S.A.

www.SullivanEstate.com

All rights reserved. No part of this publication may be reproduced, stored in a retrieval system or transmitted, in any form, or by any means, electronic, mechanical, recorded, photocopied, or otherwise, without the prior permission of the copyright owner, except by a reviewer who may quote brief passages in a review.

Printed in the United States of America

ISBN 978-0-578-01317-6

Contents

Acknowledgments		5
Introduction		7
Chapter 1	Bunkered for Life	15
Chapter 2	New Beginnings	25
Chapter 3	Alchemist Masters	41
Chapter 4	A Decade of Change	55
Chapter 5	The Man Who Dissected the World	69
Chapter 6	Living the Supreme Being	86
Chapter 7	Solomon's Ten Secrets	95
Chapter 8	The Land Down Under	109
Chapter 9	The Roaring Eighties	126
Chapter 10	Heart Storm: The Courage to Be Different	142
Chapter 11	Full-Throttle Living	158
Chapter 12	Sale of the Century	174
Chapter 13	Letting Go of the Whole	188
Chapter 14	Crisis of Faith	202
Chapter 15	The Crystal Mountain	222
Chapter 16	Liberating the Sense Pods	234
Chapter 17	Bliss with Seven Senses	250

Chapter 18	From Survival to Wellness and Longevity: A Global View	262
Chapter 19	Longevity Now	271
Epilogue		287
Literature And Sources		289

Acknowledgments

This book came alive through the encouragement of Patrick Cusick, my friend and an energetic journalist. Thank you, Patrick. Many thanks to my wife, Karin Klein-Sole, for the many hours spent typing and clarifying, and for being patient with me. Thank you to my editor, Katie Weisberger, for understanding my vision.

I gratefully dedicate this book to the important teachers of my life—some of whom are still alive, and some of whom are deceased: J. Krishnamurti, Suma Ching Hai, Helen Menock, Bert Hellinger, Frater Albertus, Paul Kroedel, Pierre Elliot, Hans J. Reimers, Johannes Klimke, and Gertrud and Heinrich Fricke.

I thank those who helped to form and shape my life experience:

My family: Thora, Erin, Sophia, Jonas, Ulrike, Robert, Palma, Sabine, Harald, Gabriele, Gerda, Gustav, Christa, Heinz, and Kaete.

My friends and helpers: Vladimi Bosniak, Robert Schweig, Gabriele Wagner, Charlotte Schwenzner, Baldur and Karin Zehle, Darell Lewis, Weibei Chen, Hans, Jill and Bill McGilvray, Werner Nawrocki, George, John, and Margret.

Martina and Uli Krueger, Greg and Kai Richardsen, Waldi and Walter and Maria, Al, Jens, Greg, Werner, Mariana and Anthony, Julica, Erika, Claire, Hermann, Mark and Theresa, Karen, Woijtek, Alan and Vikki, Bernd, Karl, Horst und Brunhilde, Margot, Matthias, Susie, Sabine, Framhild, Mike, Christine, Anita, Bill, Annchen, Lisa, Caroline, Neal, Susie and Miles, Gabriel and Antonella, Lisa and Dirch, and Marcello.

I thank Claire Scobie, Journalist and photographer in Sydney/Australia and my travel companion in Tibet, for permitting me the print of some of her great photos in this book, especially those from Mount Kailash, the camp, and others.

I thank you all from the bottom of my heart for being in my life and therefore a part of this book!

Introduction

"Just pick up what God put in front of your doorstep," a teacher told me thirty years ago. I laughed: she is feeding me a clever line like I used to feed my audiences in thousands of public lectures, workshops, trainings, and meetings. After experiencing difficult and sometimes dangerous situations courageously and consciously, I finally understood her. I had climbed the "dangerous hills" of Taoism, and had reached the wisdom and clarity to face future challenges.

I am more than a Libra born with a Leo Ascendent and Chinese Monkey traits, with illusions about being somebody special and important. I have become thoroughly convinced that I am more than just the sum of my parts. I have literally climbed nine mountains, emigrated from Germany to Australia with a family of four small children, used ancient and organic techniques to grow and extract healing herbs, started a global cosmetic-wellness franchise, and successfully sold it after twenty years. But this was not enough; eventually I had to find inner stillness. I learned that I had to just let life happen.

At age thirty-three, I diverted my seemingly foreseeable future as a spiritual guru and environmentalist prophet, opening the door to a relatively normal life of working and learning. As a result of my path, by age sixty I gained some wisdom that I am now able to share without egotism or the ambition of being a guru.

It was on my sixtieth birthday that a turning point occurred; 2004 was my Golden Monkey/Wood year in Chinese astrology. In Buddhism and Taoism, one's birth sign—monkey in my case—repeats every twelve years under a different element of the five: wood, fire, water, metal, earth. The cycle completes itself in one's sixtieth year and (usually) occurs only once in a lifetime. It occurred for me in 2004. Before then, my life had been dominated by twelve- to fifteen-hour days of work, and family time with my wife and four children. I emigrated from Germany and founded and owned a company in a foreign Australia. Success came parallel with inner work, learning, pain, and sorrow.

My experiences in the high mountains of Tibet in September 2004 finally made me aware of my restless, noisy, and self-destructive mind and my compulsive and mechanical patterns. So began my final path to self-discovery. Since then, professional work has eased up and inner work has came to the fore, allowing me to build a whole out of all the knowledge and experience I have accumulated. I stepped from intellect and knowledge to wisdom and surrender—now I have finally gained the strength to go with the flow.

Everything began to look easy; I no longer had a physical goal to be achieved, "no path to truth."

Now I am certain:

"The whole is more than the sum of its parts."
"As inside, so outside; as outside, so within."
"A little knowledge is a dangerous thing."
"There is no imagined god out there."
"Money in itself is not bad. It's what we make out of and with it."
"Do not lose your marbles."
"Hu hu is followed by ha ha."
"Enter the dragon pool looking for the tiger." This means that one must use difficulty, danger, and the challenges of life to develop strength, firmness, balance, and harmony.

To find inner peace, I had to sacrifice my dreams and illusions of being more famous, playing a bigger role in public, inventing the best life-enhancing elixir on earth, becoming a billionaire, and being admired by important people. But once peace was found, it became evident that those dreams would not actually contribute to my happiness or freedom. My thirst for inner knowledge and genuine wisdom has continued fervently, and I have become increasingly able to share it with others.

I took calculated risks and trusted myself when stepping outside my fearful, inherited, bourgeois comfort zone, gradually lifting my courage, inner confidence and trust in myself and others. I refused to gamble with money, drugs, people, and feelings. At some stages, I took larger risks and steps, financially and with unfamiliar teachers, gurus and women. I took chances in travel and relocation, and challenged my artistic, intellectual, mental, and psychological abilities.

All of these pursuits—healing through nature's secrets, alchemy, chemistry, psychology, philosophy, religion, literature, classical music, painting, wealth, society, geography, history, yoga and sports—all were unavailable from home, and not found in high school or university. I had to find them on my own and learn through teachers, gurus, books, and travel. Further down the road, I had to take my knowledge, digest it all, and make it my own. Only then could it be used to benefit others. This goal seems to be my path in life and the reason I wrote this book.

What can I learn, practice, and contribute in a lifetime? A great deal, collective and personal ego tells me. But reality says nothing! Everything has existed before. We are nothing compared with the mysterious cosmos and the infinite intelligence behind it. We may call this intelligence God, Being, Cosmic Wisdom, Spirit, or something else. As a human being, I am limited to perceiving only parts of it. The most I can do is find myself within it and contribute to it in a modest way.

There is space for those who want to learn and contribute positively. This book can help its readers to strive beyond popular notions of success, and toward inner values. This book can also help its readers to find the right information and knowledge to improve their lives and the lives of those around them. Despite my fears and insecurities, my windy and often scary path has shown me how to live in a sound and genuine way amidst the madness and compulsions of our everyday lives.

God/Nature/Life has permitted some sin. We would all be

dematerialized angels and higher beings otherwise. We face trial and error, and it is through this that we ever really learn. Through this process, I not only survived, but also excelled. What I have done you can do better—by taking small incremental risks and never giving up. Persistence, with trust and belief in our potential, is the most important thing. It grows daily, with excitement, love, knowledge, and wisdom.

I will not make the illusory and narcissistic suggestion that I might be a great role model; I simply hope my words impart a coin of wisdom and prosperity to my readers.

This book comprises the path that emerged throughout my life amid the seeming chaos and contradictions. I have learned from the masters in science and alternative and conventional medicine, and from artists, occultists, alchemists, millionaires, and billionaires. I have learned from big and small business owners, politicians, film and rock stars, Buddhists, Islamists, my family and friends—as well as those who have been deceitful. My trials and errors in science, medicine, cosmetics, and healing made me a successful—if atypical—entrepreneur, teacher, and company leader. I practiced courageous and faithful affirmations daily in the face of painful decision making, fear of failure, fear of bankruptcy, alienation in a foreign country, and sometimes, limited support from the people closest to me.

In my early life, I fearfully resisted leading from the front. By the time I reached twenty-four, however, I made the decision to learn how to do so. Sometimes this meant that I was to motivate hundreds of unwilling and egocentric employees, and greedy managers. But it also meant that I had the rewarding position of leading and helping the majority of people, who were more generous and grateful. I always felt responsible for their lives and families, and was willing to help when they faced daily struggles. What are the consequences or karmic effects a leader faces when he leads others under difficult circumstances? I learned with thousands of staff, customers and associates in twenty countries—mostly in the United States and Asia—how to become and stay successful and, at the same time, how to be human and understand others' painful life circumstances.

During personal and business-related struggles, I felt guarded and protected in some way, but still largely uncertain of my inner path. Later I discovered my inner faith more consciously, learning how to overcome adversities and act faster upon them. I know now that we are never alone: when we honestly ask, we are given. When we work with courage, faith and trust, when we go the extra mile to achieve something good for us and for others—as honestly as and genuinely as possible—then we are given.

Now I seem to truly have it all: financial independence (which, admittedly, circumstances could destroy any day), the woman I dreamed of, who is intelligent, giving, and beautiful from the inside out, my grown-up and independent children, some stillness within, my good health and fitness, and a sharp and inquiring mind. Still, I pursue values over material things and the individual over global power games.

We have to work on ourselves as individuals and save ourselves first—before we are able to help save the planet. It's absolutely necessary that we confront ourselves first, to make helping others an honest and a genuine intention. "As inside, so outside; as outside, so within," is the old saying that best characterizes my philosophy of life.

Courage, faith, and other traditional virtues are cosmic truths beyond religion. Sins, like envy, pride, greed, lust, anger/fear, sloth, and gluttony are all part of us, and we have to watch them in us carefully. Equally dangerous in my life were the man-made and useless negative energies and psychological torturers: guilt, worry, and shame. We all have to experience these feelings to some extent. We are able to learn and build our own healthy essence by overcoming their destructive force.

By facing and transforming these negative behaviors *now*, we may awaken our awareness of them and their traps so that we may stop falling into them. We are equipped to tackle all the dramatic challenges of life when we become self-aware and conscious of the real world around us. Well-being and longevity start in the Now—with mindfulness of the body, mind, and psyche, as well as an awareness of the collective issues with family, friends, society at large, and our ailing earth environment. We must practice this awareness now—or there will be no true change for the better in the future.

Violent and mindless movies, reading, following others blindly, or believing any unchallenged theory or doctrine—all these practices are worthless compared to the power of eternity, universality, infinity. These things can provide guidance or hints, but only *you* can fully awaken to your true self. There are crutches that can teach one to limp, but one has to discover for oneself how to walk and run.

I am grateful for the obstacles and challenges I have faced because they have afforded me a measure of understanding. I hope open-minded individuals will relate to my experiences of seeking the essence, harmony, and balance of life. What ultimately counts is what and how we learn from wise people—from our family, our true friends, and our soul mates.

It is my hope and aspiration that this book is bigger than the sum of its parts. Enjoy!

CHAPTER 1

Bunkered for Life

I was born inside a bunker during a night of bombing, in the small North German town of Salzgitter. Its soft green hills lie within a short distance of Braunschweig city, a primary cultural and industrial target that was regularly bombed by the Allied forces. At the time of my birth, it was the autumn of 1944, when the tides of war had turned and the defeat of the German Reich was inevitable.

My first childhood memories were those of enormous suffering. I can clearly recall my early impressions of life were of extreme hunger due to food shortages. While everyone was appalled by the wounds inflicted worldwide on the armies, navies, and air force personnel, it was the prospect of starvation that occupied most people's minds. Most families were desperate to get enough to eat. My mother, and all other women who survived this terrible conflict without severe wounds, labored for years clearing the roadways by carrying away broken bricks and rubble from destroyed homes.

My father was a Stuka fighter pilot who was captured by

Russian defenders in Stalingrad. As the Germans advanced toward Stalingrad, the Russians defiantly tied down the Fourth and Sixth Panzer armies. The battle cost Germany about two hundred thousand troops, which effectively ended the German offensive and turned the war in favor of the allies. They applied the same strategy as Genghis Khan some seven hundred years ago—by using bad weather and vast, endless territory to their advantage. Somehow, my father survived Stalingrad, escaped from the Russians, and was sent by the German army to France. Later he was taken prisoner on the western front at the age of twenty-five. Once captured, he was sent to intern in prison camps—first in Belgium and then in France. Remarkably, my father escaped from both, and even managed to bring a bottle of Parisian perfume back home for my mother two years after the war ended.

But by the age of twenty-six, he was beaten and distraught, and he struggled to find any meaning after the war. He never recovered from the mental trauma of his experience and lived the remainder of his life submerged in a numb twilight zone, fearful and shaken by anxiety attacks. Like so many others, he suffered from a depression that worsened when he confronted the full extent of the Holocaust. I remember in 1948 when he showed me photographs of bones in ovens and of starved and desperate prisoners who were freed by the allies.

The war broke the backs and hearts of the stoic people of Braunschweig, whose proud heritage dated back to the twelfth century. It was then that Duke Henry the Lion made the city the capital of his empire. He built the Braunschweig Cathedral, the most historic of the many buildings to be destroyed during months of all-night carpet bombing. Heavy bombing destroyed portions of the Altstadt (old town), which contained a large ensemble of architecturally unique, half-timbered framework houses. By the end of the war, most of the city's churches and many of the public buildings, railways, museums, bridges, and theatres were completely destroyed. .

And yet through the hardships of living in a dispirited war-beaten country, I was given valuable lessons—most importantly, an understanding of how people handle suffering. The horrors of war aroused my initial interest in a better way of life, holistic health and well-being—an interest that was later to become my passion, creativity, and livelihood. Little did I know that such immense human pain would be the catalyst for firing me into a world where alchemy, philosophy, and herbal elixirs would let me unearth nature's secrets and would send me on a fascinating journey of health, longevity, and wealth.

As a young boy coming to grips with life, my only experiences were the harsh reminders of a world at war. Reality proved to be a great teacher. Fortunately, I survived this horrific period of human history relatively unscathed, both physically and emotionally. But the tragedy also fostered within me a desperate determination to bring about change—a determination that would alchemically turn scarcity into abundance, suffering into happiness, and, most importantly, ignorance into knowledge and wisdom. Some ten years later, I would learn that alchemy is the science of transformation on all levels of life and being.

In the period just after the war, conditions in Germany were appalling. The transport system had been completely damaged, causing major problems for the distribution of even some basic goods, including food. Nearly every German city with a population of one hundred thousand or more had been severely bombed; throughout Germany, thousands of bombs had produced four billion cubic meters of rubble. The buildup of rubble, particularly in town centers, caused the carriageway to be only about three feet wide. Every city had the same first priority—to clear the rubble. I can remember taking my first tentative steps among the bomb rubble of my town. Since most able men were held in prison camps for many months, it was left to the army of women to clear the mess from the roadways and houses, all of which were in various stages of ruin.

Children had very little schooling in the first year after the war ended. Yet despite the hardships, my first three years of life provided a secure foundation for my life ahead as a healer, chemist, alchemist, herbalist, naturopath, and producer of the finest health-care products on earth.

I can clearly recall my boyhood admiration for the broken soldiers who returned home with gaping wounds and disabilities. I can also remember the awe I felt for the voluntary male and female medics who attended to the wounded on the front lines. Many disabled soldiers later confided that the medics were the true heroes of peace. These people made themselves available to everyone as pseudopsychologists and tried to reduce all the suffering inflicted on others.

Although it was painful to hold the psychological suffering of so many, the active medic didn't dare show his inner pain publicly.

What struck me at the time (and, in hindsight, sharpened my insight into the value of having dedicated healers in times of peace and war) is that all humans—soldiers, medics, rich people and poor alike—experience fear of death and sorrow as a natural human condition. I was a young boy, and the atmosphere after the war turned me into a quiet, modest person. I introspectively carried the personal and collective pain of all the victims of war. Unfortunately, Europe has a long history and cultural appetite for warfare and conquest.

When I look back on the early years of my life, the war and its aftermath presented to me a firsthand experience of the extremes of human behavior. This left me with a perpetual feeling of fear and an intense dislike for wars and injustice. It seemed so obvious to me that in times of war people suffered even more than animals.

Today, when I look objectively at people in horrendous conflicts, I realize that some people can temporarily control their fear and sorrow and others lack the ability to do so. Later on, a CEO in an herbal-pharmaceutical company I worked for told me that I had developed such a soft heart for humanity, while being locked inside invisible steel armor, so that only those close to me would know my real self. It's true that such armor can block our sorrow, suffering, and pain and allow us to overcome fear temporarily when in threatening situations. Like the quiet and noble medics who went straight to the front line and seemed to do the impossible, they hid their feelings, pains, and fears. Eventually, however, the emotional armor has to come off, revealing beneath it sadness and depression—just as my father suffered for decades after the war was over.

During the American Civil War, more than 50 percent of soldiers admitted to hospitals died. During World War I, it was 8 percent. And in World War II, 86 percent of those injured in battle died during hospital treatment.

But away from the battle zone, food shortages left families weak and barely able to survive. The expulsion of about twelve million Germans from Poland and other areas added enormously to the shortages. For weeks at a time, food was in such short supply that any homegrown vegetables were treated and protected like precious jewels.

After the end of the war—when I was almost three years old—I can remember the screaming of my grandfather Heinrich Fricke and the total despair of my mother, Gerda, and grandmother Gertrud. My grandmother had spent months devoting herself to growing essential vegetables in the garden behind our dilapidated house. They were all devastated to find out that their vegetables had been plundered in an overnight raid by thieves—just a night before the vital crop was due to be picked. We ate forest berries and roots for weeks.

In terms of lives lost and material destruction, World War II was the most devastating war in human history. What began in 1939 as a European conflict between Germany and an Anglo-French coalition spread to include most nations of the world. In the last stages of the war, two radically new weapons were introduced: the long-range rocket and the atomic bomb. However, the war was fought primarily with improved versions of weapons used in World War I, causing greater destruction and millions more dead.

The statistics show that it was the greatest war in history in terms of human and material resources expended. Some sixty-one countries with 1.7 billion people, three-fourths of the world's population, were active participants. The war's chaotic sweeps of destruction made uniform record keeping impossible. Governments lost control of the data, and some resorted to manipulating it for political reasons. A rough consensus on the total cost of the war has been estimated at more than one trillion dollars at the inflation rate of 1950, which makes it more expensive than all other wars in history combined.

Although the United States spent $241 billion, including $50 billion for lend-lease supplies, that amount does not come close to being the war's true cost. The USSR lost 30 percent of its national wealth, while Nazi looting and Russian revenge retaliations resulted in incalculable amounts of plundered wealth being taken from occupied countries. The full cost to Japan has been estimated at $562 billion.

Germany committed its entire human and economic

resources to the cause of domination, with little or no distinction between combatant and noncombatant. The human cost, not including the more than five to six million Jews killed in the inexcusable Holocaust, is estimated to have been fifty million dead. Twenty-five million of those people were in the military, and thirty million were civilians.

The USSR suffered the heaviest human losses with more than twenty million killed. The military deaths of both sides in Europe totaled nineteen million, and in the war against Japan, totaled six million. The United States, which had no significant civilian losses, sustained 292,131 battle deaths.

The Second World War should be seen in the context of other, less publicized conflicts that had horrific death tolls. For example, Stalin's twentieth-century Soviet War killed twenty to forty million Russians and Mao's "freedom wars" against capitalism killed seventy million to one hundred million Chinese. And then, there were the Korean and Vietnam wars, and, more recently, Afghanistan and Iraq. Humanity is burdened with a collective debt for all the killing and suffering caused by all wars. This debt has yet to be repaid or healed on a psychological level.

As the war years began to fade away, people's perceptions of the conflict changed. The Cold War emerged between the United States and the Soviet Union, marking a new phase in psychological war that resulted in massive spending. Life from 1947 onward improved considerably as the economic miracle known as the "Wirtschaftswunder" resulted in Germany rapidly becoming the second most powerful economy on the planet.

My early years in life were marked by the extreme polarity between nature and steel. Farms with beech and oak trees surrounded my hometown, but four kilometers away were the tall, steeplelike chimneys of massive factories that made steel for cars, bridges, railways, and building construction. These same steel plants were used very efficiently by Herman Goering Werke to manufacture weapons during the war.

While in those days there was no worry about global warming or about the environmental impact of human-made emissions, I could sense the damage being done to the air around me. The dirty coal that fueled the furnaces created an unhealthy veil over the entire landscape. As a child, I remember seeing the nightly spectacle of the glowing iron ashes being dumped on the hills far away.

My grandfather taught me that humanity needed technology and civilization to evolve, but that the true essence of living—and healing—was contained inside the human spirit and in pure nature. He would take me up to the surrounding hills to collect herbs and berries in the forests, and along the way, he would explain how every illness could be cured by nature. "You just have to know what to look for," he would tell me. Much later, I would learn from Paracelsus, the alchemist and founder of modern science and medicine in the sixteenth century, that a healing herb could be found for any sickness within a one-kilometer space (if nature was intact).

After two horrible wars, there was little medicine available, and only a few people, like my grandfather, knew where to find the healing herbs of nature and how to heal and assist others in need. I now know that the closer humanity gets to earth and nature, the more integrated life becomes. The truth is that every action is synchronized as part of a great, infinite force—a force known in many Eastern cultures as the Tao, and known in the Western world as God.

CHAPTER 2

New Beginnings

By the time the 1950s arrived, the mood in Germany had changed from that of total despair into hope, and gradually into a genuine optimism that the dark days of two horrible wars could be left behind and replaced by a new beginning. While this confidence took time to seed and grow, I found my own new beginning close to home.

I was captivated with my grandfather's faith in herbal healing. He took great delight in passing down his wide understanding to me. Under his tutelage, one of the first tasks I naively mastered was developing a sense of scent that would guide me deep into nature's treasure chest—and later into my innovations and inventions. Today I can recall from my early childhood the smell of peppermint, chamomile, eucalyptus, and wintergreen oil, as well as formic acid from forest ants. Current aromatherapy and physiology research asserts that the human limbic brain stores and recalls scents that have been experienced in early childhood.

The first thing I learned—and remembered for life—was

how to use the scents of flowers and herbs to identify them, along with their natural medicinal value. For example, the forest chamomile herb that induces sleep and relaxation and is anti-inflammatory could be easily identified, not so much for its small leaves and flowers, but by its exquisitely mild scent that soothes the mind and body.

My grandfather taught me how to identify the scents of the green, blue, yellow, and white heads of therapeutic flowers that bloomed wildly in the European spring and summer. Each of these flowers provided essential healing essences after they were extracted or distilled with care, with what was then primitive equipment. I was taught how to crush the pale blue flower petals called kornblume, along with a mixture of other plants, into an exotic concentrate that can provide sweet flavoring for food, liquor, ice cream, and even candy. We also searched for the bitter herbs like tausendgueldenkraut, a small, modest herb that grew in shaded soil among the rocks. We dried and prepared it to make a digestive aid, an important natural medicine during the early postwar years, when vegetables and fruits were scarce. People survived by consuming roots and grains not normally fit for humans. Potatoes were the staple diet—when they were available.

This practical course in hands-on forest herbalism included learning about the complimentary growing technique—known today as companion planting—where certain types of flowers, herbs, and vegetables live and thrive together. Endless talks with my grandfather in the surrounding hills and forests intimately acquainted me with an array of roots, leaves, cloves, and seeds that would be dried and crushed for the preparation of a full menu of natural medicines. We used all sorts of dried flowers for herbal teas and added a variety of freshly grown spices to the limited food available. From an early age I was shown how nature's bounty could be sought and utilized in my day-to-day life.

One of my more important tasks was to gather bunches of flowered orange marigolds that were excellent for the treatment of infections and skin disorders caused by lacerations and bullet holes. Arnica is the best herb to heal the heavy bruising that was common in combat, but it only grew well in the remote mountain land of the Black Forest. Because it was so difficult to find, I learned of a fine substitute for the rare Arnica. Bellis perennis (Gaensebluemchen) grew in plentiful quantities everywhere.

My grandfather and grandmother were living examples of how people can disengage from the suffering that abounded at the time. At the same time, they possessed an almost mystical engagement with nature and held an unwavering belief that nature contained all the secret knowledge for how humanity could transcend the evil of war, into a better world. They believed that God, found in nature, was the organic source of everything important and the caring provider of all the things that were necessary for a modest life's satisfaction. At the time, Heinrich and Gertrud Fricke appeared to me to be proof that in a savage world, goodness still exists.

Before I reached seven years of age, I had acquired a basic understanding of how to collect and grow wild herbs for a variety of natural medicines. Within a three-kilometer radius of my grandfather's home, we found just about every medicinal herb that could possibly be needed for preventative medicine. Sadly, it's not so simple today, as greedy consumers have plundered and polluted nature's environment. Those early years of hardship probably shaped me to become a pioneering environmentalist, a persona I first manifested when I took to the streets in Germany to protest against atomic waste and deadly toxic chemicals like DDT. I joined the first postwar green movement to protect the earth.

My nonviolent approach was tested in the mid-1960s, when a backlash against the protests resulted in violence and death on the streets. While flower power was the rage in the Western world, including Germany, a portion of the new generation turned to murdering politicians, bankers, and prominent business people. They were known as the RAF terrorists and were led by such names as Baader, Ensslin, Meinhof, Mohnhaupt, and Klar. They were generational heroes to some and villains to others. While some were attracted to violent protest, I supported the majority who were appalled by war and human savagery. Instead of more conflict, I went straight to nature, sought natural remedies, and searched for solutions in the force that shapes the universe.

Most people sought permanent jobs during this period, but I turned my full attention to establishing a career in natural medicine. I was not thinking of the business benefits, but I was convinced that naturopathy was the best way to heal the most suffering—both mental and physical types. These early foundational years sharpened my understanding of how natural ingredients could be used for powerful medicinal purposes. Much of this knowledge helped me to later establish Jurlique, the international company based in Australia that used herbs along with vegetable and fruit extracts to create a popular range of health and beauty products. From my early teenage years onward into my career as a scientist, I was convinced that health resulted from what could be grown organically. I was also convinced that scientific testing would eventually prove the value of natural medicine on a person's well-being.

I learned early to make teas and tinctures, using alcohol to extract the herbal essences from plants. This left a concentrated liquid that could deliver rapid results upon consumption, if taken in the correct quantity. Wines are also fermented from a variety of fruits. A modern myth says only grape wines cause hangovers. The truth is that all fruit wine can cause headaches and bodily discomfort, which can be directly attributed to the concentration of sugar, alcohol, and other substances extracted from the skin and seeds of grapes, as well as the added sulfur dioxide. It had been known for centuries, and was so well articulated by Paracelsus, that everything is a question of quantity.

Having been introduced to herbalism and basic alchemy, I already had a strong affinity for natural substances. But once I reached my teenage years, I was also drawn to science and developed an unusual determination to carry out experiments involving chemical reactions. What aroused my interest in chemistry, physics, and mathematics was a rare almanac that was handed down to me by my father. The book contained material about botany, zoology, chemistry, physics, geography, weather, and the universe—all with a simple excellence. It also published some intriguing pictures of ancient alchemic distillery practices that involved the mystifying transformations of material substances. Such knowledge was little known at the time (or even today), and this appealed to my insatiable appetite for finding new ways to work with nature.

Before I knew it, I had embarked on the fast track to a greater alchemic interest that would change my life forever. At barely fourteen years of age, I created my first makeshift laboratory in my parents' apartment, where I foolishly conducted an experiment with sulphuric and nitric acid on a small table. The resulting explosion of hot acid spilled all over the carpet and burned my clothes and face, leaving some scars. Once I could, I hid them with a beard that I still grow today.

Not only did this wayward experiment dent my budding pride, but it also dented my family's meager budget. Like all the other families in our neighborhood, we were living on the poverty line, and clothing and carpets were scarce luxuries.

That naïve and reckless experiment almost destroyed my appetite for alchemy. My parents were finally forgiving, however, and I persuaded my mother to allow me to continue studying chemistry in our cellar in a less dangerous way. She knew that I would persist and gave me a last chance when she said, "Next time, you just make sure before you do something that you are better prepared."

From May to October, my grandparents' cellar was filled with apples, pears, dried plumbs, raisins, and other produce that was picked in season. My grandmother Gertrud had a good working arrangement with my grandfather Heinrich. He was the grower and she was the processor. The way my grandmother went about selecting, arranging, preserving, and storing produce for winter was close to perfection. With simple equipment and hard work, sometimes day and night, she single-handedly manufactured all the goods for winter. Perhaps she was my role model for developing formulas and manufacturing natural products for Jurlique and other companies decades later.

Gertrud always had an assortment of fruits and vegetables bottled in jars and cans that were piled up beside the cellar walls. Bottled vegetables were essential food for surviving the long, cold winter months. However, our cache of preserved produce was extra special in that Heinrich didn't just grow fruit and vegetables, but he also added herbal ingredients that made raw material both delicious and beneficial for the digestive system. I also learned from Heinrich some skills and tricks to preserve products with nontoxic preservatives. He never divulged his secrets outside the family. When asked he said gruffly and with a smile, "Know how nature works—then you know what to do."

I liked to probe my grandfather for information while he sat in front of the fire at night. However, all he would mutter before falling asleep in his chair, fully exhausted form a long day's work, was something about never reaching the destination unless you first embark on the journey. I was still very young and not too sure what he was talking about, but I sensed that what he was saying indirectly was that a lot of learning lay ahead in my life. What I did know was that I was lucky to have learned some healing basics from someone who deeply understood nature and how humans fit into the natural mix.

Between the end of the war and the liberating 1960s, I grew from being a fearful boy into a shy teenager. As a kid, I considered poverty to be the normal way of living. Then, the concept of abundance was a word without reality. The entire region of Germany and Austria survived by growing thousands of acres of potatoes and barley. When the rich farmers harvested potatoes, they left behind some small potatoes in the soil that could be collected by the poor people. Poverty is such a degrading way of eking out an existence and can permanently affect the way people perceive the world. That's probably why I never like to eat potatoes anymore; deep down inside my memory, neurons are forever reminding me that potatoes make people poor. Sadly, half the world's population today is experiencing a similar reality of poverty.

At the age of sixteen, I made a resolution to break the shackles of poverty. I vowed that if I were to continue living, I would ensure that the rest of my life was spent with enough money and food. I had determination and a belief that I was destined to get ahead in a difficult time. I trusted that success and abundance would come when the time was right. Everything within me told me to abandon my fears and persist in my dream for a better life. I reasoned that if these fears for my survival were only a state of mind, then I had nothing to fear. All I had to do was keep my mind free of the past, and find my own freedom and formula for success. I decided to stop the confusion caused by fear and let the future pull me forward in a more positive way. So I stayed put, learned with passion, and waited to jump when the wave of opportunity arrived.

When opportunity knocks, it often comes from most unexpected places. This time it took the form of the Cold War that would split Germany apart for nearly four decades. It started with a currency crash and the printing of new money in 1948. I can remember every adult getting forty deutschmarks—equivalent to twenty U.S. dollars—to buy essential items and kick-start the dead economy. As a new economic order settled in, I was able to observe with astonishment, for the first time in my life, the duality of poverty and extravagance.

Upon invitations to school friends' homes, I saw luxury for the first time: fantastic houses, pools and cars that, to me, were a complete revelation. When I left home at twenty years of age, my family had never owned a telephone or car.

Getting educated became my obsession. Education seemed the best way to break out of the shackles of poverty that bound me during my upbringing. By the time I reached nineteen, I had finished high school. What I lacked in material possessions I made up for with my drive for learning, and I spent all my spare time studying everything that I could. I breezed through the higher levels of education excelling in science, arts, and sports. I knew by then that there was a tangible link between physics, chemistry, and alchemy, and I was keen to explore the dynamics of natural science and philosophy.

While my mind was spinning with an unfathomable zeal to gain knowledge, the physicality of swimming provided a balance to what was going on in my head. I excelled in this active sport, winning competitions at the ages of sixteen and twenty. Swimming was not just a sport I liked. Rather, the many hours I spent swimming taught me a great deal, most notably the importance of willpower—mind over body— and developed my strength of purpose. As I swam lap after lap every day in cold water, it occurred to me that everyone comes to the planet and will leave the planet alone. I reasoned that if that were true, then there can only be one purpose to this life—and that is to live, to be alive, and to make a valuable contribution to the planet. Understanding this entirely, I vowed that I would live well and let nature take care of all the things that really mattered.

My strident quest for new knowledge was interrupted, however, when I was conscripted into the army for an eighteen-month term. The upside was that I was promoted to lieutenant officer and earned 750 deutschmarks a month, plus a high severance pay, which was a fortune at the time. I had inadvertently found a way to finance my future academic studies, and the money went straight into paying my way through university.

There, I learned more about science, atoms, and the microscopic and macroscopic building blocks of the universe. I cannot say that I learned anything very remarkable from studying the sciences taught at university, but it did provide a stepping-stone into a higher realm of knowledge, where energy was not just seen as a mathematical/physical equation but as a dynamic process that could be transformed into something entirely new. I wasn't aware of it at the time, but I was soon to learn the spagyric method of ancient and modern alchemy, a threefold process taught in times past. It was very new to me, but it was nevertheless accessible to my traditionally educated mind. During my university years, I knew intuitively that once the window of knowledge was open there could be no turning back. Consequently, I became totally committed to staying on a path of discovery that had no boundaries.

After the army, I signed up for a chemistry degree that was scheduled to normally take eight long years to complete. By collaborating with a friend and study partner, we successfully condensed the time and completed the degree in four years. I then went on to do a PhD in biochemistry and physical chemistry, which included physics, chemistry, and mathematics. At twenty-six, I had attained a master's degree in chemistry while studying classes in conventional and natural medicine, music, arts, philosophy, and psychology. And yet despite all the intensity of my exhausting studies, I still had a yearning to know what was actually behind matter. I badly wanted the truth but didn't know where to look for guidance.

I wanted to find a living alchemic master who could help me to study and understand the few alchemy texts and reprints that were available from the middle ages. These texts included fairy-tale images with knowledge hidden within them. I could not find any deeper explanations in the field of contemporary science, a field confined to experimenting with dead matter. Contemporary science has little knowledge or interest in the force of life, which seems to form and direct all matter.

After my successful master's degree, I could have gone to universities like Harvard as a well-paid researcher. But I had become disillusioned with contemporary science, politics, economics, and the new social establishment. It was plainly obvious that with enough money and power anyone could buy any scientific, economic, and political result. Even Isaac Newton practiced alchemy before facing ridicule and eventually renouncing it. Little has changed over the centuries.

Regardless, my learning experience with all sciences and philosophies always brought me back to natural medicine and forest herbalism. My grandfather's legacy left me wanting much more than what science, university, and the establishment—or even pop culture and the green movement—could offer. But while I knew that I had to eventually break free from the narrow-mindedness of dualistic scientific thinking, I still had an overwhelming desire to apply traditional physical science and chemistry to naturopathy and alchemic practices.

Such idealistic thinking could be seen as a lost cause in a world that has made few advances over the past fifty years in understanding how and why people get sick. Conventional medicine took decades to scientifically link cigarette smoking to lung cancer and heart problems. Now we are reading about scientific findings that contend processed junk food causes obesity, premature aging, and death. Yet so-called soft drinks—the famous international sodas like Coke and Pepsi—are still sold as safe refreshments despite being loaded with several tablespoons of fattening corn syrup, refined sugar, caffeine, and harmful chemicals. It is amazing that powerful lobbies can get away with killing ten to twenty million people per year worldwide by oversupplying such unhealthy ingredients.

It is even more disturbing that, on average, a person in the Western world eats sixty kilograms of unnecessary chemical additives each year in the various forms of artificial chemicals, sweeteners, colors, and preservatives. And while there has been a proliferation of health foods and organic consumables in all countries, considerable scientific and political confusion exists over what is organic. Most of the labels are designed to confuse rather than educate the consumer. It's not by chance that product ingredients on food and cosmetics are as difficult to read and understand as the fine print on legal contracts and insurance policies.

In the 1960s, there were some successful attempts to link conventional Western medicine with holistic medicine. In the West, such practices emerged as ancient Ayurveda, Chinese Medicine, homoeopathy, naturopathy, herbalism, aromatherapy, and sound and color healing. Some alchemic knowledge appeared in print, and I seized it like an elixir. But when I tried to reconcile contemporary science with alchemy and traditional herbal treatments, the whole unification process fell apart and made no sense. What was missing in contemporary science was knowledge of transformation and of nature's life force.

Finally, after seven years of going nowhere in academic and private studies, as well as in work, I realized I had come to a dead end. Just as a thunderbolt occurs when a dark cloud gathers, I became aware that all the past conditioning that affected all my present thinking could never see the truth or find the secrets of nature. It seemed that the only way to progress forward was to engage nature through alternative practices such as organic farming and the manufacture of holistic natural products, along with a new process of thinking and inner experience different from the accepted one. I reasoned that by simply living and observing without judgment, I might be able to find some qualified person who could assist me in finally unlocking nature's secrets within myself

What followed were the happy, liberated days of the 1960s when the concepts of lasting peace and unconditional love were engendered in societies worldwide. I had run the gamut of conventional learning and turned to the popular mood of the time for inspiration—"if it feels good, do it." I left the materialistic establishment for seven years and helped to set up an alternative community based on the harmony of nature and the teachings of Rudolf Steiner. Steiner's knowledge of bioenergetics and life force still remains timelessly relevant.

No one believed that such a community would last forever, but that was never the intention. What really mattered was the coming together of like-minded young and old people who were living, working, and celebrating communally. This style of living created some valuable space and time for evaluating what had been achieved and for considering the choices that lay ahead. In those days, before the realignment of ruthless consumerism everywhere, the future for humanity seemed much brighter.

What resulted from our community were new products created in an environmentally friendly manner, a satisfying spiritual and artistic approach to daily life, organic farming, and unpublished, secret literature. Eventually we were not only personally fulfilled but also publicly respected. We developed the first free private school in Germany that was nongovernmental and nondogmatic. The state authorities permitted it, even though they may have mistrusted the alternative movements that were seen as rebelling against the rising middle class after two destructive world wars.

However, the idealism that sparked alternative action eventually lost track and I found myself treading a singular path with my own approach to holistic health, well-being, abundance, and wealth. Eventually the desire to find the missing links for a truly fulfilling life totally eclipsed the need for a happier place to live. I was willing to let go of all ambitious and illusionary dreams. I made the decision to search for a man known as the "master alchemist."

Dr. Albert Riedel, along with a dedicated group of admirers, held regular meetings in the Austrian Rauris Tauern Mountains and other places in the world. I was told that advanced alchemy was taught and practiced during his meetings. Most of those who studied under Frater Albertus, as he called himself, had a background in chemistry and natural medicine, and I felt both comfortable and privileged to be able to join this fellowship of learning.

If anyone knew how to unearth nature's secrets it was Frater Albertus, a spagyric master and healer who reportedly was the recipient of sacred knowledge, passed down from the great Albertus Magnus. This thirteenth-century alchemist was denounced by the Roman Catholic Church for possessing "demonic powers" that could transform metals into gold and herbal substances into a life-extending elixir or stone. His work included research into longevity and eternal youth—the dream of humanity for thousands of years. I asked myself what was fact and what was fiction and determined to search out the alchemic truth. I decided that nothing was going to stop my endeavors to unearth nature's secrets.

CHAPTER 3

ALCHEMIST MASTERS

In the thirteenth century, the Roman Catholic Church banned a book entitled Doctor Universalis. It was a lengthy manuscript purportedly penned by the great alchemist, philosopher, and clergyman named Albertus Magnus. Although its whereabouts are no longer known, the book was understood to contain all the alchemic knowledge of the period. The church called it heresy. During the same century, another alchemist, a bishop of the Dominicans Order, oversaw the distribution of alchemic and homeopathic medicines. These contained miniscule amounts of herbs, flowers, and plant concentrates that, when digested, empowered the body's immune system to heal itself.

From ancient times, an organization of brothers and sisters has always passed on knowledge of herbal healing properties. Although this knowledge would be mostly confined to the world of healing arts, the rulers of the day were also obsessed with the reports—mostly unsubstantiated rumors—that alchemical masters of the time were making gold and precious "philosopher stones" from metals, plants, and rocks.

Rulers and kings imprisoned famous scientists and alchemists in elaborate laboratories and forced them to make gold and priceless elixirs for longevity and youth, and to satisfy their insatiable appetites for sex and gluttony. The alchemist code prevented them from complying with these demands, and the alchemists instead invented an elaborate array of medical substances and metallurgy concoctions. These ultimately provided the base knowledge from which modern science took its roots.

It is therefore arrogant, foolish, and ignorant for contemporary scientists to accuse such knowledgeable people of being charlatans. Science would be almost nonexistent now had it not been for the alchemists who worked long hours in dangerous times to pave the way for the scientists of today. Rather than attacking the honor code of past alchemists, any criticism, if warranted, should be directed toward some of the modern scientists, military, politicians, churches, and religious zealots and sects that are the real charlatans.

Today the Internet is filled with a great deal of information about alchemists past and present. In the 1960s, such knowledge was not known and was often kept hidden and secret. Unfortunately, the situation has now backfired. In today's information age, the most essential wisdom is drowned by too much electronic and printed material. Just like in the past, it is not easy to find the true history of alchemic teachers and masters.

I was fortunate to find a guiding light that kept me away from distorted alchemic truths. In 1973, through the deep connections I made during "my Rudolf Steiner period," I was granted an opportunity to study in Dornach, Switzerland. There I discovered several old books in the late Rudolf Steiner's library that related to alchemy. They led me to Alexander von Bernus's book, *Alchemy and the Healing Arts*. When I received a secondhand copy of the manuscript, I read and studied it many times over. This valuable information made up for the nonexistence of a known "king of alchemy" in the twentieth century. To my satisfaction, I later discovered that, on several occasions, Von Bernus had asked Rudolf Steiner for advice on alchemy as well as on homeopathic and natural medicines.

While no king of alchemy existed, one could say two alchemic crown princes lived in the latter part of twentieth century. Both were Germans: Dr Albertus Riedel (1911–1984), often called Frater Albertus, and Alexander von Bernus (1880–1960). These men, who were both regarded as highly experienced in natural medicine, met only once. Both practiced alchemy on a higher level for many decades. They manufactured herbal medicines, healing lotions, creams, oils, and tonics by using special alchemic techniques of transformation, working out of their laboratories in Europe and the United States.

I had the good fortune to learn from Frater Albertus personally. I traveled to his mountain enclave in Austria for two weeks every year for intense study and laboratory practice, thereby completing the seven-step course over a seven-year period. This was a fascinating school, where new and previously hidden knowledge of the past three thousands years was taught openly. Truths were unveiled about alchemy as well as science, astrology, Kabala, and Sufism.

There was a certain amount of rivalry between the two alchemists. Alexander van Bernus started a very popular alchemy and homeopathy company called Soluna in South Germany. He seemed to have found secrets to better health and longevity, a claim "proven" by the fact that his wife died in 2005 at the ripe age of 101 years. While von Bernus was making a reputation through his highly valued commercial products, Master Albertus was in Salt Lake City. He set up a college there for alchemic apprentices and students, as well as a company called Paralab that produced alchemy-based products. He became known in the United States as "the alchemist from the Rocky Mountains," which is also the title of one of his books. Although authoritative in his manner and knowledge, he also showed himself to have a brilliant mind and a lot of wit.

During that time, I joined Wala, a German herbal medicine and cosmetic company, as a leader of research and development. I worked with the late Dr. Hauschka, who founded the company. I was told the company was based on alchemy and the teachings of Dr. Steiner. But, in fact, I knew much more than they knew. I was under the illusion that the company had deep knowledge about alchemistic practices. It was my personal experience, however, that the group was generally sectarian and dogmatic.

Despite this disappointment, I quickly rounded off a sound grasp of the concept of alchemic transformation through the courses with Frater Albertus. My childhood dreams with my grandfather were now being realized, and I found myself on a renewed spiritual and scientific path toward what seemed to be the final destination.

Many interesting personalities gravitated together with Frater Albertus in the Rauris Mountains every year. There were bright men and women, both young and old, who were expert teachers and students on Mahayana Buddhism, Yoga, Numerology, and Taoism. There were pharmacists, medical doctors, scientists, martial arts specialists, teachers, professors, psychologists, househusbands, and housewives. High up at sixteen hundred meters in the invigorating cold mountain air, Frater Albertus had selected the perfect place for teachers and students. We were all committed to learning, with a focus that involved locking ourselves away from both the outside distractions of everyday life and the inner distractions of our conditioned and confused minds.

Everyone eagerly assembled to learn from Frater from morning until late at night. Some processes in the laboratory had to be watched constantly so as not miss dramatic changes of substances, color, heat, and smell that occur with in vitro chemical reactions over a long period. After exhausting day classes, we would all gather around a fire and exchange viewpoints of all those matters that the mind could never understand only rationally. Those were enlightening times indeed.

During these courses, I became close friends with other students who had interests in yoga, tai chi, and psychology, and I was introduced to the first Western-trained Buddhist Lama in Europe. One fellow student, Werner A., a leading pharmacist from another famous anthroposophical, herbal pharmaceutical company, was forced to practice his alchemy incognito. His company would probably have fired him had they known he was working with Frater Albertus on such "spooky" things as alchemy.

I also met another friend, Dr. Werner Nawrocki, a medical doctor, who received alchemy advice from Frater Albertus to commercialize spagyrically made "Oil from Eggs." Eventually, after Frater's death, Werner courageously continued some of Frater's work and produced alchemic formulas for healing purposes with his company Alpha & Omega. His book, published under the name: Tranformation, Alpha&Omega, 1990 contains a great deal of advice for a practical and spiritual life that is based on alchemy.

During our studies, beginners were taught the importance of the *spagyric method*. The word *spagyyric* stems from the Greek language—*spao* means, "I separate," and *ageiro* means, "I reunite." The spagyric method involves a threefold process and various techniques to treat and transform plant, mineral, and metal matter. The three steps are expressed by symbols called *sulphur, mercury,* and *salt* (which are not related to the chemical substances of sulphur, mercury, and salt). For alchemists the symbols have multiple meanings—they can mean a substance and/or a procedure.

The first process for herbs is steam distillation, and it is used to extract pure oils from fragrant plants. The second step is fermentation or a liquid extraction, while the third step involves ashing and calcination of the extracted herbs or other substances. All three substances obtained by this separation method undergo a further cleansing process before the three factions are skillfully reunited. From the original herb, one ultimately creates a totally new, transformed, higher plant substance that may be used for medical or other purposes. A similar process is applied to metals and minerals and is taught to advanced students only.

The spagyric process is unique in its three steps of separating, cleansing, and reuniting and can be applied to all areas of knowledge, science, and life. This became an everyday practice for me to overcome daily problems with all matters of substances, thoughts, and feelings and problems with political and social systems, relationships, and individual people. We have lived for two thousand years in a time of ego-centered greed and destruction, caused by the duality of being either right—winner—or wrong—loser. Spagyric is a threefold, efficient approach to heal and overcome the painful and destructive process of dialectic reasoning based on bias and polarization, fighting and opposition. Since ancient times, the three steps to transform matter and mind were taught in mostly secret societies and to elite leaders.

Throughout European history, alchemy procedures were involved in the inductive experimental science that became allied to metallurgy, pharmaceuticals, biology, industrial chemistry, physics, and biochemistry. In Asia, alchemy has been mostly confined to a system of mental and spiritual meditation techniques in which the body, mind, and spirit are seen to exist elementally and harmoniously as one holistic unity.

One of the first questions beginners ask is, "What is transformation?" As an answer, Albertus used a typical chemical reaction to explain that, in every chemical process, substances are forced to react with each other, normally resulting in an exchange of heat. After the reaction, the resulting material has no similarity with the initial substances. For example, if elemental sulfur is heated with air and oxygen, the by-product is a characteristic flame with all the solid sulfur disappearing and turning into an acrid-smelling gas called sulfur dioxide. The original and resultant substances no longer have any similarities to one another—one form has changed into another form; a transformation has occurred. The lesson learned here is that every chemical reaction is a transformation of substances accompanied by an energetic exchange involving heat, light, or another form of energy. The same applies to more-complex spagyric processes that involve plants, metal, and minerals.

What is also often discussed in alchemic teaching is the difference between transformation and transmutation. In transformations—physical, psychological, or mental—one can follow and logically understand, measure, and explain the process of a reaction from beginning to the end. Substances can be observed easily and analyzed as they transform. In transmutations, gaps and sudden changes occur which cannot be understood with logic or any known means. One stage of existence disappears, and another unexpected one arises. For instance, we do not understand the transition from crude metals into gold (although evidence suggests that a few alchemists knew the secret). This is an entirely different, mysterious process from physics experiments involving radioactive metals, wherein small amounts of gold atoms seem to appear after bombardment with other radioactive matter.

Another example of transmutation is the evolution of life as seen in plants, animals, and humans. Many theories—or more correctly, hypotheses—abound, but none answers why or how fish turned into land animals, humans, and birds. Unknown steps or gaps occur in between; one stage disappears without trace, and another one appears. Transmutation is often misused by biologists and misunderstood in the context of evolutionary theory. Charles Darwin's framework of laws is incomplete, while the alchemy praxis and method of thinking applies interdependently to many diverse fields.

The present chaos in all areas of life could be overcome and solved by using the threefold spagyric approach, which is nonlinear. Edward de Bono introduced the term *lateral*, or parallel, thinking in the 1960s. This method has similarities with the ancient, nonlinear spagyric process. The alchemists of old avoided all problems of mechanical causation by simply looking into the nature and identity of an individual substance, inquiring into the links between the different forms taken by each substance. Consequently, links throughout all of reality bare relevance to alchemic study. Relationships between human beings, nature, and the cosmos became of critical and extreme importance for the development of alchemy.

The middle of the yearly course in Austria took place under the full moon in May—an important event which is known in the East as the Wesak Moon. In ancient history and mythology, this was a holy day to celebrate, meditate, pray, and enjoy the fertile explosion of nature, when seeds burst forth into full plants. Around Wesak full moon day, classes were more intense than at any other time. Special spagyric procedures in the laboratory compared the results of the same work at different times of the year. By maintaining the consistency of all other experimental parameters, we could clearly see the influences of season as well as the influences of constellational movement.

Modern quantum physics now knows that the experiment can't be separated from the experimenter who influences the outcome with his presence. In the same way, proof and evidence exists of how the sun and moon, along with other planets, influence the growth, structure, and quality of plants. We should not express any rigid skepticism toward the effects that planets and cosmic influences have on the matter and energy on earth.

Albertus always started every class in the morning, afternoon and evening with an ancient saying: "A little knowledge is a dangerous thing!" My interpretation of this was that no matter how smart and educated we might be, in the grand scheme of how things really are, humans know just a little. Nevertheless, we stumble around, fanatically believing that humanity and science knows it all. Under the tutelage of Frater Albertus, we all soon realized how limited the mundane human mind is. We are far removed from the cosmic interactions in which planets are connected to their families of moons, stars, galaxies, constellations, and the hidden cosmic energies that go far beyond most common knowledge. The same applies on a microscopic level to atoms, molecules, and subatomic elementary particles like protons, neutrons, electrons, positrons, electromagnetic waves, and radiation.

The courses with Albertus caused me to become very modest and humble in my thoughts and feelings, which left my mind wide open for new ideas to enter. Every day he wore the same type of woolen vest, but of a different color—for example, on Tuesday he wore red and Sunday, yellow. I have since learned that the colors related to those of the planets and the human system, as in Kabalistic numerology, astrology, and other cosmic schools of thought. Frater was also extremely charming and won over everyone with his creative intensity and enthusiasm for the truth. Through the spagyric experiments in the lab, we learned to truly see the details of the transformations and transmutations that took place. Because we are conditioned by our upbringing, we have to relearn how to see the forest for the trees. We must learn how to be present and not blinded by past knowledge and experiences, which our mind has since distorted into fixed opinions, dogmas, theories, and beliefs. We have to overcome our limited thinking to open the way for new observations, inventions, and innovations for the benefit of all.

Alchemy has one root and many branches. It is based on Egyptian sources that were adapted during the Middle Ages in Europe. These sources also formed the basis for modern science, including chemistry and pharmaceuticals. Frater Albertus taught the Kabalistic tree of life to explain the macroscopic and microscopic realities of nature. He drew on the esoteric Judaic tradition because it makes it relatively easy to understand the significance of numbers, which build the universe. Civilizations have used specific numbers and proportions in constructing magnificent buildings like the pyramids and Middle Age churches. Albertus taught how herbs, minerals, metals, animals, planets, galaxies, human anatomy and physiology, molecules, and atomic parts are all linked and interconnected with each other. And as Albertus saw it, numbers, and the essence of numbers, were the cosmic glue that held the universe together.

If Frater Albertus had one human weakness, it was his admiration for women. Quite often, he would talk about the dangers of repressed minds and feelings and he certainly did not hold back on impressing his female admirers. He was not alone in his view, as is evidenced by many of the spiritual movements in the last decades of twentieth century. Gurus like Bhagwan Shri Rainish, later known as Osho, taught admiring new age thinkers, hippies, and greenies the value of sexual freedom to overcome harmful conditioning and unhealthy obsessions with sex.

Albertus did write in his books that every person on the planet is destined to find his or her other half, or soul mate. The unfortunate reality for Albertus was that he seemed to have too many other halves in different locations. Once the affected women exchanged information with one another and found out they were not as special as they thought, the revered Albertus lost a great deal of respect from his female students. But this one blemish in his character—a trait often shared by leaders in powerful positions—should not diminish his teachings. Indeed, all modern-day people who practice alchemy hold them in the highest esteem.

In my last meeting with him, in his college laboratory in Salt Lake City, I tried to comfort him. I said that we are all humans and everything can and will be understood and forgiven. I told him not to have any regrets and to understand that he had unselfishly contributed to make ancient alchemic knowledge accessible to people with eager minds in the twentieth century.

When Jurlique was being courted for having the "purest skin- and health-care products on earth," I often thought about those seven years I journeyed to the Rauris Tauern Mountains to learn with one of the rarest and best-known alchemists of modern times. Frater Albertus never handed down his full legacy to any one individual, but at one point, he offered me his succession. I felt honored but declined modestly, knowing that I was following a different path in life. I knew that this ancient knowledge had to go through a transformation in the twentieth and twenty-first centuries. And while I could not see the goal—and who can?—I could see the signpost directing me on my personal path.

We live in a time of hyperspeed information exchange, and excessive published knowledge. Any secret or occult form of alchemic or other teaching—including all exchange of communication—must be able to adapt and fit within with the new world of IT. As a qualified modern laboratory scientist, I was clear and certain that ancient wisdom had to evolve into a more public arena. I knew that alchemy would always flourish in any arena, wherever life thrives, whether through private individuals and families or through business people.

Along with other books, Albertus wrote *The Alchemist of the Rocky Mountains* while doing spagyric experiments and creating a commercial enterprise called Paralab in Salt Lake City. He confided to me that he could not write about all of nature's secrets in his books. "I'm not a writer," he said. "As I see it words are only the rough guides to nature's bounty." Albertus taught that reading and studying alone would not lead anyone to the destination. To think so, according to him, was an unsatisfactory illusion.

The truth I discovered as an alchemist's student for seven years was that everyone has to walk their own path and, with guidance, we can discover how to live our destinies. What Frater Albertus left behind is a legacy of valuable alchemic knowledge that lives on with gratitude in the hearts and minds of his students.

CHAPTER 4

A Decade of Change

While the 1940s were a decade of hopelessness, followed by the relatively prosperous 1950s, the arrival of the rockin' 1960s saw the first beginnings of a lifestyle that reflected the ideal of a kinder, softer humanity free from the suffering of war. Toward the end of the 1960s, I had completed all my studies as a chemist, scientist, and naturopath, and set out to commercially manufacture spagyric, organic healthcare products, and naturally derived plant colors. Changes were coming fast, and new ideas were being voiced about how people and communities could harmoniously coexist. The views were many and diverse—ranging from extreme, security driven conservatism to radical activism. Self-sufficient communities were mistakenly perceived to threaten established values.

Without this rebellious and sometimes chaotic movement toward of new lifestyles, the world would be less tolerant, poorer, and more rigidly fixated. Acceptance of change and engagement with other cultures and ideas brings transformation to individuals as well as society. This was shown after the Cold War when Russian tanks squashed a hopeful uprising of people during the "Praha Spring" Hungarian revolution. The creation of the impenetrable Iron Curtain and the erecting of the Berlin Wall also instigated this type of change. Out of this brutal repression a new generation evolved called the '68ers—a generation to which I belonged. This generation began to disagree with their parents who had become fearful and uptight because of all the guilt and pain that remained after the long war. They sought comfort from their sorrows in material things—higher incomes, some degree of luxury and fancier titles—but they could not be blamed.

The new baby boomer generation that had not experienced the hardship of war resisted the cold war mentality. We simply rebelled on the streets against what was at first a sense of helplessness, and later against the aggressive politics, police, government, and laws that limited human rights and freedom. We rallied together as a mass of environmentalists, greenies, and idealists who loosely sought free market trade without either polarity of either the capitalist or communist system. The hippy revolution, along with drug "researchers" and pop music culture, struck a chord with the breakaway German youth; the Beatles got their first huge fan base through concerts in Germany.

Meanwhile, the older generation, the survivors of a war-torn nation, watched speechlessly as a small minority of young, and mostly academic, protesters, turned violent. They killed bankers, politicians, secret agents, and business leaders.

A boiling point was reached when planes were hijacked and the culprits ended their lives by committing suicide in high security jails. The last Red Army Faction (RAF) terrorists were prosecuted in the 1990s, and the first offenders were released in 2000 after long prison sentences. A huge sign erected in 1968 in front West Berlin University, a school heavily influenced by socialism and communism, characterized the end of the 1960s with the words, "We are against everything." Similar movements, mass demonstrations, and street actions happened in France, Italy, the former Czechoslovakia, and other countries. Some naively idealized Ho Chi Minh and Che Guevara. All of this has been well presented in a 2008 film, *The Baader-Meinhof Complex*, which has aroused vivid memories and painful emotions in the now-mature generation of '68ers, as well as in the older generation.

In an ironic twist, some of those protesting youth who once threw stones at police made it to the highest offices of Government Ministers. They formed the core of the popular Socialist and Green parties that directed German government policies in the 1990s. What a transformation it has been from the ultraconservative situation that existed immediately after the war.

The 1960s and 1970s were also the days when Eastern mysticism fused with the materialism of Western culture. Cults and sects sprung up everywhere, in all countries across Western Europe and America, and conspiracy theories abounded about communist infiltrators corrupting Western youth with drugs, unrealistic promises, and covert brainwashing. In Germany, the pop culture arrived from the United Kingdom and the United States, and while people didn't dance in the streets over it, inside the bars and clubs, a new generation of idealists and optimists was born.

The new generation indulged in all the momentary sensations that were readily available. While hedonism thrived on the energy of rebellious and loud rock music, the early 1970s saw a number of cults and sects explode onto the youth culture. These groups gained power mainly using mind control and thought-stopping techniques such as chanting, and these experiences were sometimes heightened by the use of drugs.

A peaceful weapon used by sect leaders was love bombing, which discourages fears and doubts and reinforces the need to belong. Shree Raineesh, also known as Bhagwan (and called Osho after his strange and mysterious death), lived, preached and practiced ways of overcoming sexual fear and conventional conditioning. To combat centuries-old boundaries, he instructed students to let all restrictions go and indulge in free, wild sex orgies in groups and with multiple unknown partners. These orgies were often accompanied by the hype of the guru, numbing metal music, and hallucinogenic drugs.

The Transcendental Meditation movement, founded by Maharishi Mahesh Yogi (1917–2008) in India gained hundreds of thousands of followers across Europe and the United States by promising to teach Yogic Flying, in addition to meditation techniques. Yogic flying is a levitation ability supposedly achieved through meditation. Unfortunately, the practice proved to be more about body mechanics and physical yoga training than spiritual ascent. While genuine meditation, used daily, is generally advantageous for mind relaxation and changing one's perception of life situations, the plethora of trance methods used by members of various sects were not so authentic or enduring.

To the contrary, the practices basically disabled critical thinking skills, and created a somewhat debilitating internal experience. If they could not escape early enough, members eventually felt victimized by the guru, and cults thrived by encouraging their members to become dependent and childlike. They operated on the principle that the best way to separate a person from his traditional culture of association is to apply techniques that disorient a person's critical and logical thinking, as well as his or her common sense.

Most people who joined cults that mushroomed in prosperous Western cities were New Age seekers who were recruited by friends or family members. The first imported cult to hit Europe and the United States was the Moonies in the late 1950s, followed in the late 1960s by the Hare Krishnas and the TM movement (of which the Beatles were followers). Some of the more dangerous cults preached apocalyptic endings, which resulted in such tragedies as the self-immolated Branch Davidians and the self-poisoned followers of Jim Jones. These more dangerous cults came under the world spotlight when the U.S. heiress and cult member Patty Hearst killed a man while she robbed a bank.

The late 1960s and early 1970s were a raw time of extreme

naivety—a mishmash of a freewheeling, hedonistic lifestyle and a birth of new generational ideals. After years of study, I wanted to find my part in this new world, and I looked for inspiration from those teachers who had shown through their writings, workshops, and actions that they knew the way to a better world.

While studying spagyric medicine and alchemy in the Austrian mountains, one name stood out as the doyen of developmental, evolutionary, and transformational knowledge. That name was Rudolf Steiner (1861–1925). Among his many achievements, Steiner left the world a legacy of biodynamic organic farming and an exceptionally progressive educational system known as Waldorf or Rudolf Steiner Schools. He also contributed greatly to the areas of science, meditation, and art. Today the Rudolf Steiner schools are thriving in most European countries, North America, Australia, New Zealand, and Asia. The longevity of the schools is a testimony to their revolutionary philosophy that continues to change the way people view education all over the world.

It was Paul Kroedel, writer, speaker, artist, and dedicated anthroposophist, who became my next teacher. Kroedel had met Rudolf Steiner personally in the 1920s and translated Steiner's sometimes-difficult spiritual language into more modern language. He also possessed an intimate understanding of Steiner's social and educational ideas. Through Kroedel, as well as through my later experiences living within a community based on Steiner's ideas, I have learned a great deal about the life and mission of this man.

Rudolf Steiner was born in the former Yugoslavia in 1861 and grew up in an area south of Vienna, Austria, called Wiener Neustadt. He was the son of a village stationmaster, and as a young teenager, he demonstrated an insatiable thirst for learning. By the time he turned twenty, he was an accomplished linguist, classicist, mathematician, scientist, and historian. While he demonstrated a zeal for traditional learning, he quickly turned his attention to spiritual matters and became involved in the Theosophical Society of London, which at the time was bridging Eastern and Western spirituality. Based on these beginnings, Steiner founded the Anthroposophical Society in Germany. This institution fostered the development of spiritual science—a field applicable to scientific, artistic, and social life—that occupied most of Steiner's energy for the rest of his life.

Steiner fought against racial, gender, and social discrimination, and predicted many of the current global developments and problems fifty years ahead of time. Through his pupils, he desperately tried to persuade the Kaiser in Berlin not to partake in the upcoming First World War, and warned of the danger of an ensuing Second World War. He clearly saw both wars coming and predicted them well in advance. Steiner also foretold that an insane man would take over the new, vulnerable, and idealistic German democracy, and that his leadership would be as ruthless and brutal as that of Lenin, Stalin, Genghis Khan, or Temur.

The beginning of the twentieth century saw a renaissance in science and technology, and Rudolf Steiner determined that education should be based on spiritual and factual truths as opposed to the values of capitalistic greed or communist conformism. This led him to assist in starting a company called Weleda, which produced alchemy-based homeopathic and herbal medicines in the 1920s. Along with the new healing medicines he created, Steiner also developed a new system of crop planting called *biodynamic agriculture*, which was the (superior) precursor to the modern organic movement. This new system of agriculture started in Europe and has since spread globally. His knowledge is finding a valuable place in the world today, when deforestation and the spreading of dangerous chemicals such as herbicides, pesticides, and fertilizers are destroying the planet's farming ecology.

Rudolf Steiner was also a prolific writer and lecturer. I was once the proud owner of his printed writings and lectures, which totaled some three hundred volumes. These books were color-coded in rainbow hues, each marking a different area of his contributions to humanity. Steiner gave knowledge and practical advice unselfishly, to the point of personal exhaustion. He was an incredibly charismatic figure, a formidable intellectual, an active artist, and a spiritual role model.

After the First World War, Germany underwent a revolution. In 1919, when the Kaiser abdicated his throne, the ruling class was swept from power. Steiner decided that this was the appropriate time to start a movement that would establish the foundations for a new system of economics, government, and rights—one based on justice, compassion, and fairness for all. His Threefold Social Order of economics, politics, and culture was a revolutionary transformation of the three ideals of the French Revolution into a working reality. This was significant in that everyone would be accorded equal rights in everyday life matters—*equality*—freedom for all people in spiritual and intellectual pursuits—*liberty*—and finally, brotherhood and sisterhood in business life—*fraternity*. Steiner's method, as in the spagyric process, was to separate the three ideals of the French Revolution, and then relate and restrict them to different, new areas of the social organism. In this way, he was then able to correct the ideals of the French revolution without alienating the best minds of his time.

Steiner's personal standing meant that his movement met with immediate success; industrialists grouped together to merge their factories into an economic enterprise based on Steiner's principles. Eventually, however, the Steiner idea of threefold equality, liberty, and fraternity ran into opposition from established groups. Realizing that a reactionary tide was arising, Steiner turned his attention to a special training course for schoolteachers. He personally created new curriculums and helped to convert school buildings while simultaneously lecturing and attending meetings for parents and teachers. He also traveled throughout Europe to initiate more educational and social reforms, and gave thousands of lectures to people from all walks of life. Some lectures were only for laborers.

Though a wonderful teacher, Steiner refused to be seen as a prophet or to see others as such. When the spiritual leader Krishnamurti was advertised by the Theosophical Society as a future Maitrea Buddha, Rudolf Steiner fled from his former involvement with the organization. He firmly stated that the godly status attributed to Krishnamutri was nonsense. Krishnamurti later agreed with Steiner, and left the Theosophical Society to follow his own path.

Steiner died of being poisoned in 1925, at the age of sixty-four. At the time of his unfortunate and much-too-early death, his schools were operating successfully. When the Nazis came to power, however, all the schools were closed. During the years from 1930 until 1960, Steiner's ideas of spiritual values and learning systems fell out of fashion. Instead, the world searched for solutions through materialism and new mechanical and electronic technologies. But with the winds of change that swept through the Western world in the late 1960s, there arose a renewed interest in Steiner's brilliant ideas and advances.

The basic Steiner concept was that all education should be based around how a child develops physically, mentally, and emotionally. In his system, children are encouraged to fulfill their full potentials, but are not to be pushed too early toward intellectual goals that adults often impose on children. His approach was reflective of what he had learned from being a master of "spiritual science." As a philosophy, spiritual science is the opposite of rigid, uncompromising mechanistic science.

I was educated as a Steiner schoolteacher and a high school teacher, and learned all about what differentiates Steiner schools from those in the mainstream. Up to the age of seven, in Steiner schools, children are encouraged to play as much as they like; they draw, paint, tell and listen to stories, study nature, and use all-natural materials in the process. No child younger than six or seven is forcefully taught to read or write, and when they are taught, writing comes before reading. One teacher instructs the same class of students for seven years, and therefore, develops close relationships with each student. Teachers fully engage with each child, and ensure that they are enthusiastic about all the materials being covered. They teach ethical behavior in the classroom, but not a strict set of beliefs. The demand on the teachers' skills is very high.

After their first years in school, children are encouraged to concentrate on one subject at a time, such as history for two hours per day for several weeks. Then, for instance, the student will move on and focus on geography for two hours per day for several weeks. This approach prevents the fragmentation and confusion that results from teaching too many intellectual subjects at one time. Specific time is always set aside for mathematics, sport, arts, and music (each child learns to play an instrument). Students are encouraged to find links between arts and sciences, and genuine learning is encouraged—not just studying for specific tests and exams. This attitude subdues or ends the worries that students often have about learning.

Four of my five children attended a Waldorf (Steiner) School in Germany and later on in Mt. Barker in South Australia. For a child to spend his or her first years in a Waldorf School is still the best option for early schooling. I have observed Waldorf graduates to excel in traditional universities in all subjects including medicine. If the system has one weakness, it is the high school curriculum. The main reason for this is that Steiner died before he could provide his ongoing input and correct teachers in their practice. While Steiner was an idealist, a tireless educator, and a diligent artist who never compromised his beliefs, he was also a down-to-earth pragmatist. He modified the school curriculum to ensure that the children covered the same subject matter and attained the same skills as children in other, more traditional government schools.

In addition to his enormous contributions to education, Steiner was also an architectural genius and an outstanding teacher of what Pythagoras termed "sacred geometry." He explained how the point, line, and plane represent the first three dimensions, but that a kind of reversal of space is involved in the ascent to a fourth dimension. This theory has still not been scientifically proven. No one has been able to match—let alone expand on—Steiner's brilliant construction of a fourth-dimensional hypercube. In architecture and sculpture, he introduced the "double bent geometric plane." He created models of alternative energy-transforming machines, which were akin to a Perpetuum Mobile.

He was surrounded by highly skilled academics in astronomy, medicine, pharmacy, and the arts. They all desperately craved the deeper knowledge and skills that Steiner freely and willingly taught. Steiner boldly led those who were interested into a world of hidden extra dimensions. He explained his ideas with words, diagrams, analogies, and examples of many kinds. In doing so, he was able to demonstrate that human objectives and everyday thinking were the low rungs of a ladder reaching up to infinite heights.

Today Steiner's teachings of human existence have been translated into many languages. They continue to manifest tantalizing new and still untapped horizons of awareness. They are increasingly relevant to our time as our planet becomes more interdependent and increasingly threatened by man-made causes. In particular, his discussions of the relationship between scientific studies and the development of direct perception of spiritual realities have attracted renewed attention and admiration from a new generation of knowledge seekers. Steiner's books and printed lectures are garnering big hits on the Internet.

Rudolf Steiner's message was undoubtedly one of the biggest inspirations on my life. He was one of the few people that left me speechless and overwhelmed. In the 1970s, I helped to found a teacher community in Reinstorf, Northern Germany, based on the spiritual, business, and social ideals of Steiner. We were comprised of up to thirty people in and were called Herder Seminar. We thrived for a few years educationally, artistically, and scientifically and contributed to society with our viable business endeavor that was based on the spiritually of Steiner's educational ideas.

While Steiner showed the way for the practical applications of much known knowledge—with progressive education poised as the key element for creative sustainability—the full picture of enlightened understanding had still to be painted. For this to happen, there needed to be a living person who was free of dogma and the burdensome baggage of the past. What the world desperately needed was a new spiritual leader after Rudolf Steiner's death. And so, from the debris of disenchantment and disorder, came a shining "Star of the East" who was conscious and experienced enough to avoid being labeled a prophet: Jiddu Krishnamurti.

CHAPTER 5

The Man Who Dissected the World

I met KM—officially known as Jiddu Krishnamurti—at a special gathering in 1985 in London, shortly before he embarked on his farewell lecture to his homeland of India. In that same year, some eight months before his death at the age of ninety, he spoke to the United Nations in New York and was awarded the UN Peace medal.

The extraordinary appeal of Krishnamurti—to rich and poor, religious and atheist, hedonist and naturalist—was a phenomenon of the twentieth century that many believe rivaled the "coming" of Jesus of Nazareth and the future arrival of Maitrea Buddha. However, KM totally rejected this notion. He instead preferred to teach the knowledge of how human "prisoners" could free themselves from the cages of their unwanted and compulsive thoughts.

George Bernard Shaw declared the humble modern-day sage the "most beautiful human being" he had ever seen.

Krishnamurti's many friends included Aldous Huxley, mythologist Joseph Campbell, artist Beatrice Wood, physicists Fritjof Capra and David Bohm, writer/philosopher Iris Murdoch, and the Dalai Lama. Psychotherapists representing various theoretical orientations, including Freud, Horney, Sullivan, and Rogers, met and held discussions with Krishnamurti, a person they greatly admired.

He was, and is still, considered a great teacher—if not the greatest—by many diverse religious and philosophical figures. Although Krishnamurti had a special admiration for the peaceful Buddhist monks, he disagreed with all rituals and traditions as he contended they "caged humanity." "We are not meant to be caged," he said, "as we are evolving beings with a living physical body that is connected to a freely thinking mind and metaphysical substance."

Twentieth-century Gnostic philosopher and occultist Samuel Aun Weor spoke with great praise for Krishnamurti's teachings, going so far as to say he was a "highly realized Buddha." Gurdjiev, the Russian guru of Eastern spirituality in the 1940s, said that KM was the only human being in the twentieth century who had attainted the state of self-realization, or enlightenment, by transforming his mind and thought-feelings, without being initiated by a living master.

In one exchange with the spiritual master Anandamayi Ma, Krishnamurti was asked, "Why do you deny gurus? You, who are the Guru of Gurus." Krishnamurti replied briefly, "People use the guru as a crutch." Krishnamurti lectured to the Indian Prime Minister, Jawaharlal Nehru, telling him,

"Understanding of the self only arises in relationship, in watching yourself in relationship to people, ideas, and things; to trees, the earth, and the world around you and within you. Relationship is the mirror in which the self is revealed. Without self-knowledge, there is no basis for right thought and action."

Krishnamurti was much more than a spiritual teacher. He displayed a unique ability to dissect the intellectual processes of the mind, and was able to explain, quite succinctly and with absolute certainty, how humanity perceived the world. On several occasions, he also revealed some astonishing observational skills by being able to correctly disassemble and reassemble complicated memory associations. He could also fluently articulate the mechanisms for dissecting thoughts and feelings, and then alchemically reunite human awareness with a hidden creative source.

My purpose for meeting with Krishnamurti was to see him in the flesh and hear firsthand his global and personal outlook, which included a vision of the whole earth, humans, and the universe as distinct from its parts. I discovered that his understanding of life and the world was holistically pure and free from all prejudice and past experience, thoughts, and feelings. His warnings of ecological retribution came long before the clear and present dangers of global warming, horrendous pollution, and climate change filtered down into humanity's consciousness.

Krishnamurti often spoke about his concern for the human impact on the environment. He asserted that because the human species was a part of nature, yet did not care for itself or nature, nature would eventually implode back onto humans' ability to live and evolve. According to Krishnamurti, the only way humans could coexist harmoniously with nature was through right education and the development of an affinity between all people, so that any problems affecting nature and humanity could be resolved amicably without conflict. The communion between nature and people was spiritual, asserted Krishnamurti, as the energy of life is always free and never lonely or limited. His message to humanity was that everyone had to think and act differently in the present to affect any real changes for a better world.

Among his "teachings" was the assertion that that the human being is already perfect, and that any attempts to change or mould nature's holistic unity of body, mind, and spirit by action or technology was an act of pure and simple violence.

As an alchemy student, scientist, and seeker in search of pure knowledge, what impressed me most about Krishnamurti was his ability to dissect the world and then put it back together again in a powerful reenactment of creative splendor. What he demonstrated to the alchemically minded was, in fact, the remarkable spagyric processes of working with the mind.

Krishnamurti's primary teaching was that "truth is a pathless land," and that humanity cannot come to an understanding of this original truth through any organization, through any creed, through any dogma, priest or ritual, nor through any philosophical knowledge or psychological technique. The only way to possess this knowledge, that held all the secrets to life, was through the synergy of collective being. And this was only possible through understanding the contents of the mind through observation, and not by intellectual analysis or introspective forays.

A main contention of Krishnamurti was that humans have built themselves images as a sense of security—religious, political, and personal. These "mind objects" manifest as symbols, ideas, and beliefs. The burden of maintaining these artificial images, based on psychology and on the past, dominates all human thinking, relationships and daily life. People's self-created images are the root cause of all hindrances to a peaceful, happy existence. They tear apart humanity and every relationship.

Krishnamurti's revelation to humanity was that the psyche, self or mind is the energetic product of thought and feelings and, as such, had no entity or permanence. He further explained that human self-consciousness was not a thing, but a movement that could be characterized as "fascist" as it insists on its own importance and survival. In addition, he completely denied the worthiness of a spiritual hierarchy by asserting that the primary reason why people came to him as a guru was to find solutions to ease their self-created problems, pains, and sorrows. They sought to fabricate a self-evaluating spirituality and an imagined form of enlightenment.

He pointed out clearly that any belief in reincarnation or a comfortable or punishable afterlife was an illusion, and was merely a tool for the ruling churches and sects to keep conditioned people—mostly the poor—quiet and subservient. All humans are manipulated by their thought process, which is related to past knowledge, projected into a nonexisting future, and all based on "I," "me," "myself," and ego. Trying to use the mind as a thought-feeling process in the present, however, could lead to different, real, and worthwhile results. After listening to Krishnamurti speak for several days in a packed tent with three thousand people near Salisbury in England, I seemed to be suspended in space, but totally grounded at the same time. His words had an exceptionally calming influence.

At once, I found the revered speaker gently touching my shoulder and asking me, "My young friend, you look lost, how can I help you?" I was then forty-one years old, and he was perfectly fit, mentally and physically, at ninety. I somehow stuttered that I was new to this place and to his teachings, and was somewhat overwhelmed. He pointed at some people and instructed them to look after me.

I have been blessed in my life to receive and welcome at least five remarkable and highly developed human beings while journeying on my "pathless" way to truth. I asked myself, "Is it so that in every generation, people have the desire to meet somebody special to be inspired by, someone who somehow initiates self-awareness?" To my surprise and gratitude, a few months later, during his final talk, Krishnamurti answered my long-term inner question directly. In Madras on January

4, 1986, KM focused on the nature of inquiry, life, creation, and the effect of technology.

His poignant articulation went something like this: "Are we inquiring into what makes us special? What makes a bird? What is the creation behind all this? No description can ever describe the origin. The origin is nameless. This origin is absolutely quiet. It's not whirring about making noise. Creation is the most sacred thing in life, and if you have made a mess of your life, change it now. Change it today, not tomorrow. If you are uncertain, find out why and be certain. If your thinking is not straight, think straight, logically. Unless all of that is prepared, unless all of that is settled, you can't enter into this world, into the world of creation." For me, as a music lover, that harsh truth was articulated so elegantly by KM like a perfect conductor of a great symphony.

He then went on further. "How does the mind behave that functions on knowledge? How can the brain that is recording all the time see the importance of recording and not let it move in any other direction? Very simply: you insult me, you hurt me—by word, gesture, by an actual act that left a mark on the brain, which is memory. That memory is knowledge. That knowledge is going to interfere in my meeting you next time. Knowledge is necessary to act in the sense of my going home from here to the place I live. I must have knowledge for this. I must have knowledge to speak English. I must have knowledge to write a letter and so on. Knowledge as function, mechanical function, is necessary. Now, if I use that knowledge in my relationship with you, another human being, I am bringing about a barrier, a division between you and me, namely the observer. That is, knowledge, in relationship, in human relationship, is destructive. That is, knowledge which is the tradition, the memory, the image, which the mind has built about you, that knowledge is divisive and therefore creates conflict in our relationship."

I had heard all of this before somehow, in bits and pieces, but never with such clarity. In the context of the struggle of everyday life, this was first time for me that spiritual, philosophical, and religious ideas could be applied by everyone at one time. In the twenty-first century, Suma Ching Hai and Eckhart Tolle speak a similar, often easier to understand language of truth and change, which is easy to apply and practice. These ideas have become the basis for my latest travels and innovations.

With the precision of an alchemist separating the codes and messages from a material substance in a laboratory, Krishnamurti was the conductor of the orchestra of life—on central stage—explaining the interdependent sectors and functioning of the human mind. He elaborated on how the "music of the mind" can hinder clear perception and objective analysis, and can create conflict in relationships.

He explained how the brain is programmed and trained to record, because within that process of recording, we believe we find safety, security, and a sense of vitality. In the recording process, the mind creates a false image about oneself. And that image will constantly get hurt. "Is it possible to live without a single image about yourself, or about your husband, wife, children, politicians, priests, or without any ideal?" Krishnamurti would say it is possible, and furthermore, if it was not found in a lifetime (assuming reincarnation exists), then a person would continue to get hurt, always living in a pattern in which no freedom is possible.

His main point is that once a person gives up complete attention and inattention, then recording no longer happens. "It is only when there is attention that you record. That is, you flatter me; I like it. The liking at that moment is inattention, therefore recording takes place. But, if, when you flatter me, I listen completely without any reaction, then no center consciously or subconsciously records."

All that Krishnamurti said made sense, as I had long understood that thoughts and feelings were the scattered garbage of the mind. They could either be acted on or discharged back into the memory banks. However, was there something else, another interactive source that could be the first beginning thought? And if the brain and mind are the source of thought-feeling, then both the brain and the thoughts are of the same matter. What I wanted to know was how the brain and mind, with all its stimulus and response mechanisms, could remain unaffected. How could all this clutter be removed from the mind?

The answer, according to Krishnamurti, was astonishingly simple. The solution was not in preventing thought, as this would be like stopping a mirror from reflecting. Only then, there was no action, judgment, or choice involved. All that was required was to let the observer—your created self—go away. Then you can allow the thoughts to come and go naturally. What Krishnamurti was saying was that peace and stillness is simply a state of mind. No one has to oppose anything—including the coming and going of thoughts and feelings.

There are techniques for letting go of thought-feeling cycles. That, I understood, but what about guilt, fear, and suffering? What do you tell somebody who is suffering excruciating pain—physically or psychologically—that can't be stopped? And is there any point for someone who is terminally ill to put up with unbearable pain that won't go away? And what about the collective guilt and pain everyone must have, from the more than 100 million humans that have been deliberately killed by dictators and armies in the twentieth century alone?

In 1922, Krishnamurti went through a psychological transformation that resulted in a severe physical condition. This episode preempted an intense spiritual awakening that he later described as "the process." This excruciating pain led to an extraordinarily calming understanding. At the nape of his neck, a hard, ball-like mound would swell. This created extreme physical discomfort and sensitivity, as well as a total loss of appetite and occasional delirious ramblings. At one point, he lapsed into unconsciousness. He later recalled how he was totally aware of his surroundings, and during this state, experienced a "mystical union." The dualistic complement of the pain was a climactic sense of "immense peace."

By dissecting the parts of suffering and fear, Krishnamurti succeeded in being able to unite his body, mind, and spiritual being. This was possible because of compassion.

Following the pain, he became supremely happy. "I have drunk at the clear and pure waters and my thirst has been appeased. I have seen the Light. I have touched the compassion that heals all sorrow and suffering. It is not for me, but for the world. Love in all its glory has intoxicated my heart; my heart can never be closed. I have drunk at the fountain of Joy and eternal Beauty. I am God-intoxicated."

Krishnamurti continued to allow the phenomenon to occur. The "process" involved various degrees of physical pain accompanied by a presence that was often felt by those who witnessed KM. The "process" for overcoming suffering and pain was a cataclysmic milestone for the soon-to-be "world teacher." The repeated experiences of pain and enlightenment lifted a burden from his heightened consciousness and provided him with the clarity to let go of others' expectations and to allow his way of clarity to blossom for the benefit of all. He did this without dogma or the baggage of any traditional teachings.

Fear, pain, and pleasure were the ongoing themes in KM's yearly public talks in England, Switzerland, India, and the United States. While in San Diego in 1970, he explained how fear always occurred in relation to something else and could not exist by itself. "There is fear of what happened yesterday, in relation to the possibility of its repetition tomorrow. There is always a fixed point from which any relationship takes place. How does fear come into this? I had pain yesterday—there is the memory of it—and I do not want it again tomorrow. Thinking about the pain of yesterday, thinking which involves the memory of yesterday's pain, projects the fear of having pain again tomorrow."

Krishnamurti was adamant that it is thought itself that is the root of all fears and sorrows. "Thought breeds fear. Thought also cultivates pleasure." To understand fear one must also understand pleasure, as the two are interrelated. Without understanding, the duality of the thought process there can be no escape from fear. This means that it's impossible to say, "I must only have pleasure and no fear." Fear is the other side of the coin. Krishnamurti's insightful understanding is that thinking of yesterday's pleasure creates thought patterns that the same pleasure may not happen tomorrow. This very thought of "not having pleasure" engenders fear. Thought then tries to sustain pleasure and thereby nourishes fear.

Krishnamurti's one fear in life—that he eventually overcame—was that he would submit to the falsity of an exalted status. At the age of thirty-four, he publicly renounced fame and the messiah status being thrust onto him by the Theosophical Society. They proclaimed that he was the new incarnation of the Maitreya Buddha. After he rejected these claims, he spent the rest of his life holding public talks in South Asia, Europe, and the United States. He was never seduced into the trap of a guru or prophet, and lived a modest, private life.

Born into a family of Telugu-speaking Brahmins, Krishnamurti was described by his teachers as "vague and dreamy." His teachers at school regularly beat him. Later, Krishnamurti wrote about his misunderstood childhood as a period of time when "no thought entered his mind." He was watching, listening, and nothing else. Thoughts with associations never arose. No image making occurred. Sometimes, he attempted to think, but no thought would come.

When he was eighteen years old, he had a psychic experience of seeing his dead sister. In 1909, the occultist theosophist, C. W. Leadbeater, a renowned clairvoyant, told the boy Krishnamurti that he had the "most wonderful aura—without a particle of selfishness in it." Upon the agreement of his parents, KM was taken away to England. Two years later, the Theosophical Leadership established a new organization called The Order of the Star in the East (OSE) to prepare the world for the coming of Krishnamurti as a new messiah.

Expectations of the new messiah reached a hysterical point in 1914, when at the age of nineteen, he was due to visit Sydney, Australia. The Star Amphitheatre at Balmoral Beach had been booked for the "world teacher." Such was the extraordinary hype at the time that the radio station 2GB—owned by some of Krisnamurti's would-be disciples—speculated that the master would walk on the harbor water through the Sydney Heads. The discomfort felt by Krishnamurti in becoming the world's first super guru coincided with the unexpected death of his twenty-seven-year-old brother, Nitya, who battled tuberculosis for years. The death shook Krishnamurti's belief systems and, after going through yet another inner revolution, reunified his essential core and shattered all remaining illusions.

His ultimate declaration was, "An old dream is dead, and a new one is being born, as a flower that pushes through the solid earth. A new vision is coming into being and a greater consciousness is being unfolded. A new strength, born of suffering, is pulsating in the veins, and a new sympathy and understanding is being born of past suffering—a greater desire to see others suffer less, and, if they must suffer, to see that they bear it nobly and come out of it without too many scars. I have wept, but I do not want others to weep. But if they do, I know what it means."

He told the story of how the devil and a friend were walking down the street when they saw a man ahead of them stoop down and pick something up from the ground. The man looked at it, and then put it away in his pocket. The friend asked the devil, "What did that man pick up?"

"He picked up a piece of the truth," answered the devil.

"That is a very bad business for you, then," said his friend.

"Oh, not at all," the devil replied, "I am going to help him organize it."

Right up until the final second before his death in 1986, Krishnamurti maintained that truth is a pathless land, and can't be approached by any path or by any religion or sect. Truth is limitless and unconditional, and it cannot be organized. Essentially, Krishnamurti was concerned only with one thing—to set humanity free "from all cages, from all fears." Above all else, Krishnamurti believed that authority was the main hindrance to the pathless truth.

"All authority of any kind, especially in the field of thought and understanding, is the most destructive, evil thing. Leaders destroy the followers and followers destroy the leaders. You have to be your own teacher and your own disciple. You have to question everything that man has accepted as valuable, as necessary." This was what I sought. This truth would stop my blind wandering, albeit sometimes it would be jarring. It would provide me with the strength, conviction, and passion to nurture my knowledge and roots, both inside and outside.

Krishnamurti used the word meditation to mean something entirely different from the practice of any system or method to control the mind. At a public talk in Bombay (Mumbai) in 1971, he spoke on meditation and its implications at length. "A mind that is in meditation is concerned only with meditation, not with the meditator. The meditator is the observer, the censor, the thinker, the experiencer, and when there is the thinker, then he is concerned with reaching out, gaining, achieving, experiencing. And that which is timeless cannot be experienced. There is no experience at all. There is only that which is not nameable. When there is the sun, the light, the beauty, the clarity, then all these powers—developing various centers, chakras, kundalini—are like candlelight. And when you have that light, you don't want anything else."

Krishnamurti revolutionized the way people viewed the Eastern concept of meditation by saying with certainty that the only worthwhile purpose for practicing meditation was to "learn about yourself, watch yourself, watch the way you walk, how you eat, what you say, the gossip, the hate, the jealousy—if you are aware of all that within in yourself—without any choice, that is meditation."

The purpose of life was not a struggle to arrive somewhere or to transcend anything. Conscious, deliberate striving is always within the limits of a conditioned mind, and in this mind, there can be no freedom. What Krishnamurti left to the world—and the life ahead of me—was the acute awareness that the one true friend in the world was your own free mind. Life can be free of fear and struggle with the right understanding. All that is really needed is to burn a passion flame of awareness. Everything else then flows naturally.

I had to give up a path toward a fixed goal, as well as my ever-present inner struggle with my mind and feelings that resulted in sorrow, pain, and guilt. I could use the present—the now—as a tool to come closer to self-awareness. My struggle in everyday life with family, friends, enemies, and business people would go on, but in a different way. My unusual approach to health, based on alchemic and holistic well-being and self-awareness, had reached a boiling point. I realized that all the great teachers I had met along my path in life had pointed me in the same direction—my inner way. Through following my own path, I would transform old wisdom into inventions and innovations, and help others to reach better health and a new approach to longevity.

CHAPTER 6

Living the Supreme Being

Apart from Krishnamurti, Albert Riedel, Eckhart Tolle, and Rudolf Steiner, the only other person who inspired me to boldly live a life free from all fear and expectations was a diminutive Vietnamese woman. Hundreds of thousands of followers proclaim that she is the living incarnation of Quan Yin, the female Bodhisattva known to Buddhists and Taoists worldwide as the Goddess of Compassion.

When I first saw Suma Ching Hai she was barely forty-five and stood just five feet tall. The first thing that struck me was her crazy Zenlike laugh, which somehow elucidated the essence of what she was teaching in the moment. Her jovial sense of humor was cosmically infectious. She would often become intensely animated—twitching her nose, eyes, and mouth while making various contorted facial expressions. I later found out that her zany grin might have resulted from her left cheek that is slightly paralyzed.

As is the Asian way of demonstrating gratitude and reverence, her followers lay flowers, fruit, and candies at her feet and on stage at her lectures. While she accepts small offerings from the heart, she also contributes large amounts to world charity. Her disciples always give money generously, as well as labor when there is a natural disaster and people need immediate help and support. Just after a disaster, they have arrived and are already helping while big global relief organizations are still discussing and planning.

Ching Hai stoutly shuns any "guruishness" by dressing up in radically different outfits for each of her lectures. One night she might dress like a Madonna in virginal white, with a powder puff complexion, and the next day she appears in casual jeans with a trendy ring in her nose. The next occasion she presents herself in a grandiose costume with jewels of a local queen or princess. "Don't look at me; I'm just the messenger," she explains. She never takes any money for herself and always lives a very modest life, wandering to different places with her tent or caravan. Even so, she was an honored guest and speaker at the United Nations in New York.

What impressed me most about Suma Ching Hai was that she was able to "alchemically" take apart and then put together the most powerful teachings from the Indian Bhagavad Gita, the Buddhist Surangama Sutra, the Christian Bible, the Koran, and others. By uniting and fortifying the power of these sacred words and applying them to everyday life, sorrows, and fears, she was able to exude a vibration of communication. Her audience was often left delirious and thirsty more of the same wise and unlimited knowledge. Her name means "vast ocean."

The ancient teachings—along with all the new knowledge of quantum physics and multiple universes—were like "spagyric putty" in a master's hands as "the lady" created and then explained far-reaching insights using all her personal charms and wacky humor. With her penetrating, razor-sharp intellect and simultaneous compassion and insightful observations, Ching Hai always provided a spellbinding performance.

Known in her native country as Hue Dang Trinh, she delivers an uncanny and penetrating portrayal of life's truths. She is half Chinese and half Vietnamese, and grew up half Catholic and half Buddhist before the American war in Vietnam. She always invites Western people, whom she calls snowflakes, to accompany her on the podium to answer their often-critical questions. The Western mind seems to need her presence most, compared with all her admirers from Asian countries who are more content with the traditional Buddhist environment. Ching Hai speaks several languages and lectures fluently in English, Mandarin, Vietnamese, French, and German.

What I find most striking about Suma Ching Hai is her compassion for all viewpoints. Her generous nature is seen in her ability to be inclusive of those whose belief systems are most vulnerable and contradictory. In this way, she comes across as nonthreatening, while delivering a powerful statement that resonates long after she is finished speaking. It is as though a burning light resides deep inside her mind and heart, triggering the listeners' minds to feel the same way.

People have tried to tie down her teachings, but she refuses to be drawn into being part of any one dogma. She explains, "Our path isn't a religion. I simply offer you a way to know yourself." What she does offer is the basis for peace and love that everyone wants and seeks. She explains that it is already within each and every person. "The answers will come not from the outside but from looking within an uncluttered mind. We can have both heaven and earth at the same time. Why not enjoy them both now? There is no mystery about how to know God. It's very, very simple. You can see God within while you're living." Meditation for her is living in the now, allowing for the "garbage" that came in to get it out. She says, "Garbage in, garbage out."

Born in Au Lac, Vietnam, Ching Hai spent much of her adult life in Taiwan, which was where we first met. Her father was a highly respected Naturopath who was interested in philosophy. When she was a young girl, an astrologer declared that she possessed a "super noble character." From early on, Ching Hai had a close affinity with nature and could feel the pain of plants. She could never pull apart flower petals without a compelling reason. She was also known to care for many wounded animals and has always been a vegetarian.

When she turned twenty-two, Ching Hai left home and went to study in England, France, and Germany. At thirty, she met and married a German scientist. But, after two years and with her husband's consent, she left the marriage in pursuit of enlightenment, and became a Buddhist nun in India.

While in the Himalayas, she was discovered and initiated by a wise hermit into the Quan Yin technique of divine transmission, an intense experience of light and sound. While living modestly and quietly in an Ashram, she was asked by fellow nuns and monks to become their teacher. She was hesitant, shy, and resistant at first. But as soon as she agreed, the result was a spiritual avalanche that moved rapidly around the world. Millions of students as well as her initiated practitioners are always set alight by her presence.

If only one person fully understands holistic life practices and living holistically, it is Suma Ching Hai. She continues to lecture to hundreds of thousands of her followers all over the globe, and now even on Sky TV. People from all walks of life attest to her simple and special meditation technique that provides fulfillment, happiness and peace in their daily lives. With the beginning of the twenty-first century, she has had to reduce her retreats, which always attracted thousands of participants. She withdrew to avoid gatherings that were too large, and now communicates mostly through an electronic magazine. She appears only monthly, with fewer disciples visible, but it hasn't changed the adoration, gratitude, and commitment of countless followers. She says she never wanted to become a guru to the masses, and that her initiated disciples could all do what she did. She told them there was no longer the need for them to see her personally.

One of the insights that I learned from Ching Hai was her explanation that light and sound can be the special metaphysical language that can be used for higher communication. Light and sound, she explains, is the manifestation of our internal wisdom which is beyond the physical hearing or seeing. Rather it's the internal awareness of what a person creates of him or herself. The essence of what Ching Hai teaches is that the true nature of human beings is the cosmic light that shines within each and every person. In other words, when you go inside yourself you will find that "everyone is truly universal light." This reality can be personally experienced as God, Tao, Buddha, Allah, and any other entity or Supreme Being. These divinities are present inside and outside of humans—in everything, everywhere. And, according to Ching Hai, this abundance of divine essence can be discovered in the now, as it simply is.

Buddhists and Taoists worship Quan Yin as the Goddess of Compassion. According to Ching Hai, she discovered the way to harness the divine compassion that can overcome suffering in the high Himalayas. The technique she inherited focuses on the "third eye" center, located in the middle of the forehead. This, she attests, is the wisdom center and the highest knowledge gateway for the body. However, she cautions that the technique must be learned and practiced correctly, as there are dangers in concentrating on any *chakras*, or centers of energy, without proper guidance.

Ching Hai was once asked, "I feel a chill from my spine going up to my head, and then there seems to be a feeling of energy encircling in my head. What does this mean?" "That's okay," she replied. "It's your kundalini at work. Afterwards you'll be used to it. Other people practice many years to try to awaken the kundalini, and they can't do it." Focusing on the third eye chakra offers a safer method to access the kundalini, which apparently works for her students. This is evidenced by the tremendous number of personal testimonies that speak to the truth of her teachings.

An initiation into Ching Hai's enlightenment is often described as "sudden" or "immediate" enlightenment. It works this way because the initiation requires giving up eating animals, stealing and lying, and instructs that initiates must only speak the truth. Ching Hai also advises that a person wanting to find a power greater than oneself should not use intoxicants and should restrain from any sexual misconduct. "Sex can be good," she says. "But like gluttony, there can be too much of a good thing." She tells of her early sexual attachments and experiences, and she has unconditional compassion for those who seek worldly pleasures. But, she says, "At some point we all have to leave the lolly shop."

As for herself, Suma Ching Hai—a woman on a mission—maintains she is merely a transmission pole for compassion. She speaks passionately about people's needs for receiving and extending compassion. She told the Dalai Lama that he should lead the Buddhist *sanghas*, or communities, in allowing women to become fully ordained monks. And she encourages the world's leaders to commit to wiping out poverty. "There's enough money for everyone. Compassion is inclusive. Intention and action should not be exclusive."

She says she could talk for a hundred years, but the only

important role she plays is to transmit the light of true understanding. She explains that she simply teaches people what they are, and that this understanding cannot develop through words but rather by experience. It develops through a higher level of consciousness in daily meditation and life.

When asked to elaborate on the process of transmitting light, she responded, "I cannot explain it in words. It's just inside of you and me. It's just the power of God that's doing this. No talk, no language to describe that. That's why it needs a living transmission pole, otherwise all the bibles would have done the job a long time ago, and we would have been able to do it ourselves already. But the light of knowledge needs a living transmission. In every century on the planet, someone is chosen—and sometimes two or three people—to transmit this power. Whoever wants to go back to where creation begins. This transmission of light is what's known as the Kingdom of God."

I was fortunate to meet Ching Hai three times—twice in a large meeting and once personally with a smaller group. At one point when she touched my hand, I could feel her essence resonating through my entire being. Unlike the so-called supreme masters that traveled from India in the 1960s and 1970s, Ching Hai makes no demands and gives her supporters the best of both worlds. There are no initiation fees or collections from disciples. Both people and money are attracted to her as a natural condition of love and respect.

Some may jealously call her a shrewd merchandiser, as she is able to sell anything she creates including her paintings, music, poetry, aesthetic jewelry, clothing, and designs. But all the proceeds go to selected people in poverty and in natural disaster settings. She seems to avoid those famous charities that use donations to finance huge administration costs and executive expenses. She talks little outside her lectures, and is a living example of charity every day of her amazing life.

As far as Suma Ching Hai is concerned, material possessions are not the problems for humans. Attachment to these possessions is the root cause of all problems, all wars, all conflicts, and all suffering. Her solution is to enjoy life by remaining detached—clear of clutter in mind and heart—while at the same time being compassionate to those who are struggling for survival and striving for a better way of life. When you are poor, live a happy life. When you are rich, enjoy it but be compassionate: give. Money and wealth are positive energies in Ching Hai's view, and they reap goodness when used generously. She says the same thing to everyone who is willing to listen: "Share the light of compassion and you'll enjoy life so much more."

CHAPTER 7

Solomon's Ten Secrets

I have no doubt that gaining knowledge of the "Three Ms"—mind, matter, and metaphysics—can be enormously beneficial for those who are genuinely seeking a way to sustain happiness on earth. Spiritual masters like Krishnamurti and Suma Ching Hai, Eckhart Tolle, and Frater Albertus provided me with a holistic blueprint that would prove invaluable as I ventured outside of my old world. But down on earth, toward the end of the 1970s, the economic picture became blurry. Financial rules were being taken apart and restructured into freewheeling and high-rolling systems that thrived on the multiplier effect: global production made revenue, and more capital fueled higher production. The richer got richer faster, and the poorer got still poorer, as is painfully evident in the world's populations today. I saw long in advance the financial crisis of 2008 coming, and warned people I knew not to risk their hard-earned savings, capital, and other assets. The financial world of today is like a rollercoaster controlled by the super rich, and supported by mostly young and financially inexperienced investment players. They have used other people's earnings like "Monopoly" money in a global casino game based on greed, envy, delusional thinking, and lust.

If I could have foreseen the way international business would be carried out in the 1980s and 1990s, I probably would not have ventured out of Germany. Instead, I would have stayed in a safer place, working as a well-paid spagyrist, chemist or environmentally conscious product developer in a research laboratory. But fortunately for most humans, we can't see into the future and we still have to use what's called 20/20 vision: taking what worked well in the past and applying it to the present, and then directing it toward the future. There are a number of flaws in such a system, however, as it totally disregards the "now" factor—the present moment. In spite of this, the general concept of sticking to what works made a lot of sense to me at the time.

In the early 1980s, my wife and four children decided to look for "greener pastures" away from Europe. After my research in Southern France, Ireland, Western Virginia, and New Zealand, it was finally the brown, dry land of South Australia—the driest state on the driest continent on earth—that captured my attention. My mission was to find the purest possible land to grow organic herbs, plants, and flowers, and to spagyrically transform them into quality health-care products.

What was to become the trillion-dollar natural health

business twenty years later had just started to sprout; but suddenly, the financial system went into a freefall. The so-called junk bond raiders in the United States were challenging the banking system by issuing high-yield bonds to hundreds of corporations who required fast and risky cash for expansion. While the raiders secured corporate takeovers, the commercial money supplies went from being a scarce commodity into what was classified as "unlimited funny money." Something would have to give sooner or later, and I desperately searched for a winning formula that would keep my fledging business afloat if the financial world collapsed.

When I did my initial research into the fundamentals of the postwar capitalist and communist systems, I found to my surprise that most of the economic theories were either vague, contradictory or made no sense at all. They were often built on a flawed basic assumption that all of humanity should gain. Keynesian economics was the preferred system of economic management, whereby governments would keep reserves of cash backed by gold in times of inflation and would print hard currency during times of recession. By the 1970s, the gold standard had long gone, and governments would instead mark up or mark down the value of their currencies when they liked and as they saw fit. This cozy arrangement worked fine until a new breed of financial entrepreneurs decided that it was their turn to shore up the corporate money lines, thereby breaking the bankers' rice bowls while boldly encroaching on the establishment's hallowed turf. A money war was looming and the consequences of the fallout were far from certain. Conspiracy theories of the 1970s were now evident in praxis and were presented convincingly in Gary Allen's book, *None Dare Call it Conspiracy*.

My problem was that while I could sense that the capitalist juggernaut was leaking like a sieve, I had no idea from where it was leaking, and I did not know to whom to turn for sound advice on how to raise seed money for my new company in Australia. However, like everything in life, if you have the right intention and willpower, and are prepared for a diligent and intelligent search, solutions invariably come. The one truth that the seeker can rely on is that eventually the doors of knowledge will swing wide open. Fortunately, through my alchemic understanding, I got pointed to the one name in history that has been immortalized for transforming his wisdom. I discovered the ten secrets that he used to build an empire while, at the same time, acquiring huge volumes of wealth. King Solomon, son of the biblical King David, built wealth and fame and celebrated life in grand style with generous charity.

History recorded that Solomon ruled the kingdom of Israel from about 970–930 BC. He is credited with having wisdom greater than that of Eastern mystics and Egyptian scholars. He wrote more than one thousand poems and songs dealing with the duality of wisdom and folly. In his wisdom, he understood that religions, governments, conquerors, wealthy individuals, and all organizations had vested interests and were vulnerable to using knowledge for selfish gain. He dutifully wrote down his ten secrets for building an empire that would sustain abundant wealth in a healthy way.

Secret 1: Dissolve the Ego

The first secret to building a lasting kingdom, organization, or company is to connect to the universal energy source that is much bigger than the self is. Seekers need not ask for what they want but instead should be content to abandon their egos, and go with the flow. In other words, if you don't ask for what you want then you will get what you need, and ultimately will not want what you once did. Once a person drops her or his ego and connects with a higher universal power, then things just happen naturally in abundance. This fundamental secret for success in business involved direction from firm leadership, which Solomon wisely declared must "first be spiritually fulfilled."

Solomon's wisdom here is that in any business, government or empire the organizational structure will quickly fall apart if ethical standards were not implemented. The demotion of the ego and the acceptance of a much bigger universal force is the only way any organization driven by people can accumulate wealth. Solomon encouraged his traders to do business with integrity, and he was the first person to advocate this win-win principle for commercial success. The first pillar of Solomon's wisdom was not to seek glory, riches, and power but to dare to win in a fair way.

According to King Solomon, all that a person needs to become successful in life is to find knowledge and act with wisdom. Solomon used his wisdom well and was rewarded with riches, health, honor, and victory over his enemies. He asserted that all success is dependent on what a person gives, as what you give always comes back multiplied. The world economy has moved far away from this wise and logical principal, resulting in booms and busts on Wall Street. Stockbrokers gamble with other people's money, promising poor retirees the opportunity of getting rich without losing their nest egg, which most did in 2008.

Secret 2: Focus, Focus, Focus

The wise king Solomon was adamant that anyone with an idea, plan, or burning desire to succeed had to set the mission and then focus on it. When Solomon decided to build a temple for God and an adjoining royal palace for his family, he took on a huge undertaking that required precise and elaborate planning and construction skills. Throughout the years of painstaking construction, he never once lost focus despite the enormity of the task. He never forgot his intention, despite the numerous problems he encountered with carpenters and engineers who complained that what the king asked for was impossible to build. Solomon's second secret wisdom was to always think big and stay focused. When Solomon's elaborate temple and palace was completed after twenty years, visitors were astonished with the quality of the workmanship. At times during the construction, he did not have enough workers or stones, but he used what he had brilliantly, and was even able to line the walls with gold.

Secret 3: Keep on Trading

Solomon's mission of building a temple was visionary, extraordinary, and monumental, and while he never lost focus of the primary mission, he was forever collecting his internal resources for trade purposes. More prudent rulers would have not aimed so high, considering the lack of materials, skilled carpenters, and manual workers. Not Solomon, who gave his maximum effort to acquire resources by trading everything he had. Solomon was a capitalist who believed that to receive, a person, organization or empire had to be prepared to give. Solomon reaped the rewards of his aggressive trading strategy, amassing an army of chariots that he stationed in his cities to keep the peace and to allow free trade. Solomon got his chariots predominantly from Egypt and resold some of them to other countries that also needed fast transportation. His golden rule was to always seek trade for profit, which would benefit all. Goods and services traded were tangible and never created out of financial delusions, as they often are in our time.

Secret 4: Find Good Leaders and Contracts

During Solomon's reign, there were periods of conflict, wars, and dangerous political situations. Solomon's secret to preempting conflicts was to consolidate good leadership within his kingdom. He was a decisive leader, and never baulked at making difficult decisions. He expected his leaders to act—and not to spend endless hours discussing strategies and debating issues. One of Solomon's strategies was to give his enemies sufficient rope to hang themselves. For example, he told an enemy of his father, King David, to build a house and not to depart from the area until it was finished. If he left the area, for any reason, death would follow. When his father's enemy eventually left the house to join his servants in another location, Solomon explained that the agreement had been broken and ordered his opponent's execution. Solomon honored his agreements and meticulously stuck by them. He told his leaders to make friends whenever possible, but to put binding agreements on potential enemies to avoid blood, fighting, and aggression.

Secret 5: Form Alliances

Solomon succeeded in expanding his trade routes, thereby increasing his resources by making strategic alliances with friendly rulers. The purpose of alliances, according to the Solomon wisdom, is to eliminate competition by extending cooperation. During Solomon's reign, strategic cooperation was the business mantra. In modern times, research has shown that the cooperative business model engenders the "feel good" factor, and consequently brings about greater success. On the other hand, the competitive model creates fear and disharmony in the market place, which results in reduced creativity and productivity. Solomon put it more simply: live by the sword and die by sword. His solution to fighting was to build alliances, and he did this with strategic marriages and other acts of consorting to make his rivals feel at ease and not threatened.

Solomon understood the power contained in alliances. By actively seeking out partners with skills and resources, he was able to effectively mould teams that could achieve goals quickly. His most famous alliance was with Makeda, Queen of Sheba, who ruled over Ethiopia. Egyptian hieroglyphic records reveal that the Pharaohs obtained frankincense and myrrh from Ethiopia. Solomon secured trade and wealth by sealing a sexual union with Makeda that produced a son named Menelek who went on to found Ethiopia's Solomonic dynasty.

SECRET 6: PROTECT VALUABLE ASSETS

Solomon's biggest responsibility was to safeguard the Ark of the Covenant, which was his kingdom's most valuable asset. When King Solomon completed his palace and temple, he dedicated his new property to a covenant with God. As far as Solomon was concerned, the Ark of the Covenant was the passion and flame of his life that made his kingdom possible.

Today a company's most valuable asset is its ability to produce goods and deliver services that make a profit and enable the employment of staff. A company's data bank, trade secrets, patents, and contact lists could also be deemed valuable assets, and Solomon's wisdom, if applied today, would be to store them safely and not allow them to slip into the hands of rivals. If Solomon were ruling over a modern company, he would protect his primary assets by ensuring that their computers were secure from hackers, and that the company buildings had surveillance monitors and were equipped with a state-of-the-art fire prevention system.

Secret 7: Wisdom before Power

What historians have widely recorded was that King Solomon always put wisdom before power. He never failed to rule wisely even when presented with difficult and seemingly impossible decisions. The rich and poor, rulers and tradesmen, all came to Solomon with their concerns. History shows that Solomon always judged fairly and was always quick to administer justice. The famous story, in which he decreed that two feuding women should physically split apart their disputed son, showed that he was prepared to use drama and passion to bring about a satisfactory result. Solomon ruled with integrity, and while he was not averse to showing his power with elaborate celebrations, when times were tough he excelled in holding his empire together with wisdom rather than fear or bullish power. Capitalist and communist systems could learn a lot from this way of ruling.

Secret 8: Always Celebrate Successes

King Solomon encouraged his people to celebrate every success, and above all to celebrate the gift of life. When he finally completed his temple and palace, he held a feast that lasted for fourteen days. Solomon encouraged ritual as a way of acknowledging events and accomplishments. He expected his people to be thankful, positive and to enjoy life. By celebrating success, people were more content with their work, and stayed content. Celebrations were something to look forward to, and a welcome break from the daily routine that can be a perennial struggle for those who don't know how to celebrate the joy of living. Joy is always a "now" experience, while pain, sorrow, and negativity are not.

Secret 9: Live Simply

While Solomon enjoyed celebrations, he detested greed and envy. His one regret in life was that he was ultimately seduced by extravagance and gluttony, which almost brought about his downfall. After overspending on extravagances, he had to cede property to Hiram to pay his debts. In the time of Solomon, kings and queens were often victims of the foolishness of building monuments that they couldn't afford to pay for. They did so to demonstrate their power and achievements. Even the great Solomon let ego get in the way of his wisdom at times, although he always advised his friends and subjects to enjoy the simple things in life as nothing lasts forever.

Secret 10: Honor All Agreements

How was it that King Solomon was able to honor his agreements while other leaders broke theirs as quickly as possible? Solomon stood by one primary agreement that enabled him to build an empire. This was that in return for what he offered as wisdom, he would receive gifts. If the great king were alive today, this arrangement would be that in return for his expertise he would be paid a "consultant fee." Solomon was not only an idealist, and his agreements resulted from his pragmatic desire to secure his cooperation with trading partners, neighboring countries, and strategic allies.

Ironically, his Achilles heel was that he loved so many beautiful women that he began to worship them. This broke his sacred agreement to put God ahead of everything, including powerful, attractive women. Because of this broken agreement with his higher power, he lost a lot of his wealth during his final years in power. As a seeker for the meaning of life, Solomon examined hedonism, materialism, and various philosophies and ultimately decided to make an agreement with God to resist from all meaningless pursuits. His vow to God kept the door open for him to find value and then to celebrate life with passion.

Over five decades I have attended many executive seminars and business conferences that were geared toward improving human relationships, cash flow, and company profits. However, back in 1985, as the founder and CEO of Jurlique, I had read for the first time about King Solomon's ten special secrets. I shipped the first order, worth eighty-six thousand dollars, from Australia to the United States and made an agreement with myself that Jurlique would save 10 to 20 percent of all its profits as a prudent reserve, and give another 10 percent to charity and those needing support.

Because I had to start with next to nothing, the first five

years were a rollercoaster between excitement and the threat of bankruptcy. With my family of six, I lived on the brink of poverty and funneled all income back into the company. Some of my staff earned more money than I earned and drove nicer cars than I could afford at the time. I put my life and creativity into spagyric formulations, manufacturing and educating people about a new level of health and well-being. I also took great care in attending to the company's human resources, and saw to the ongoing education of staff, business stakeholders (customers, distributers, and suppliers) and myself. I strictly adhered to the secret rules of King Solomon in everything that I did during those first years.

During the Sydney 2000 Olympics, sitting in a corporate sponsors' box watching the Aussie runner Cathy Freeman win a gold medal, my accountant Mark reached over and said, "Do you know you've just got Solomon's wish and gained financial independence?" I replied with a stupid Aussi cricket expression, "How's that?" My accountant smiled and then explained, "Well that prudent reserve you've been putting aside for sixteen years—with bank interest, after paid taxes—has just topped five million dollars."

I looked at Cathy Freeman on the winner's podium, remembering well my affirmation during a challenging seminar in 1995 in Melbourne, led by Robert Kiyosaki, and muttered, "Well done, Solomon." I still could not believe it. Now was the time to overcome my poverty script that had been set in my mind. I accomplished this goal by doing something wisely and gratefully, with hard-earned money, and by avoiding the trap of power and senseless agglomeration. Despite the fact that some people have difficulty seeing me as a capitalist or a socialist, I still view myself as both a free market trader and a caring socialist, but never as a delusional Marxist, communist or reckless capitalist.

My early childhood of painful poverty, fear, and sorrow could now end fifty years later, but there were still some inner and outer challenges waiting before more joy and bliss could enter my life and remain there. My two psychology teachers, Bert Hellinger and Helen Menock, both helped me with their (sometimes harsh) reality checks. They did this so that I could finally break through the poverty barrier in my mind and with my actions in everyday life. The greatest benefit to me from Solomon's wisdom was that I was able to realize that money is a necessary good. Wealth and material possessions are not evil when they are used in the right way.

CHAPTER 8

THE LAND DOWN UNDER

In the midseventies, I began developing natural cosmetics and traditional herbal medicines full time. I worked in various laboratories in southern and western Germany. I had to run my own expanding laboratory and, while doing research, discovered that the stevia herb was fifteen times sweeter than sugar and other synthetic sweeteners. I also found it to be extremely beneficial to both the pancreas organ and the entire digestive system. Extracting stevia from the leaves of a Paraguayan tree was illegal in Europe. In the United States it wasn't possible to import the stevia plant from Paraguay, where it grows in abundance, due to FDA regulations. This action was designed—intentionally—to protect the extremely influential and powerful sugar and sweetener industry. In Japan, low-calorie and side-effect-free stevia is sold and enjoyed by a large population. This hasn't gone unnoticed by Coca-Cola, Pepsi, and other companies—they have already registered patents for Stevia Cokes! Stevia is now permitted as a health supplement, but the necessary Gras Status for common food and drinks is still delayed by the FDA and sugar-related lobby groups.

Another by-product of my research was the development of harmless, nontoxic natural color paints, along with an assortment of building materials that had no harmful side effects whatsoever on properties or occupants. The products are still being sold in all variations through three German companies, and they constitute a serious contribution to the ecological building market that is helping to create a cleaner "third skin" for earth's fragile environment and people.

Although I was achieving a fair amount of success with my research—and business opportunities were starting to open up slowly everywhere—I quickly realized that I would never be satisfied with the restrictions and impositions of work as a company research chemist. I could feel my creativity being stifled; I was basically unemployable by companies and institutions. I wanted to break free and, with some effort, was able to help establish a small company called Florin that pioneered the introduction of raw materials used to produce soymilk into Europe. Florin was also one of the first private companies to manufacture organic tofu and soymilk for retail sale, made from soybeans in Germany.

These products, still a novelty in Europe, came with a do-it-yourself kit and were distributed to the first small "green" shops. I followed the Japanese lead and manufactured soy whey, the leftovers from making tofu "cheese." As tofu and soymilk struck a chord with the rapidly emerging young health seekers, I accepted the challenge of producing the first soy whey liquid soap, which proved to be an instant hit.

My secret for processing soy whey was a special fermentation process. I later applied a spagyric variation to the formula to manufacture fermented soy-whey as a base for a range of cosmetic products. My new friend, Karl Elser, who died later in a tractor accident, was an intelligent distiller of fruit spirits. Together, he and I did the first ten-thousand-liter batch of fermented soy whey raw material, which was then a huge amount for the small demand in the marketplace.

These early successes wet my appetite to run my own race—and put into motion a vision for an international business that would successfully produce quality organic health products. I sensed that the world was looking for a whole new range of organically grown, naturally manufactured products for premium health and beauty care. I also realized very early that to succeed I would have to be the prime mover and leader of a company that would, from the beginning, set new standards as a world pioneer in the health and pending well-being industry. The challenge would be to convert the knowledge of natural health and spagyric processing into selling a range of products. These products would need to be thoroughly researched, manufactured with the highest quality control for accreditation standards, and then distributed worldwide.

Because the IT industry was still in its early stages and complementary health care was undeveloped, I felt strongly that I needed my independence to create a range of new spagyric health products. These products would fit the expectations of a more health conscious future. I could see no reason whatsoever for selling off my formulas to business speculators cheaply, and having gone through some difficult postwar years, I liked my chances of starting up a business that produced quality products. I realized early that I would have to do it all by myself. Later I had to attract skilled people who would be passionate about producing and selling the very best health-care products in the world.

But before I could get going, I needed the support of my family. Both my wife's family and my wider family would have preferred me to stay put in Germany, thinking that I was more of a philosopher, scientist, theorist, and dreamer than a determined businessman. As a close-knit family unit with four children all under the age of ten, we had always lived and worked together. We had benefited from living within an idealistic, alternative community of teachers that was engaged in biodynamic farming and Steiner's other specialties including the arts and the esoteric. For years we had studied the Steiner teaching methods for our children's and other children's education.

Many friends and family confided most sincerely that there was no future in starting a health-care company from the bottom up, but by that the time, I had already made up my mind. I was to commit my family's future to my own company in a foreign land. Quite naturally, I tried to turn other people's negativity into positive action.

On my own, I traveled to Southern France, England, Western Virginia, New Zealand, and Australia to find the right place for my entrepreneurial ideas. My first choice was definitely not Germany, Switzerland, or Austria—there was too much red tape in these governments and big sums of money were needed to even dream of a new start up. Little cash and a "can't be done" attitude in central Europe nevertheless encouraged me to accelerate our exit from a safe old world. At the time, I could see people shaking their heads, questioning how a man about to turn forty years could head off to the other side of world with his family of small children. The truth is that finally, my family of six viewed our collective move as the chance of a lifetime and I, for one, had no time for entertaining any thoughts of doubt.

By the time we decided to commit to a new beginning in a distant land, there were early signs of a worldwide health boom. Unfortunately, the difficulty in the beginning was that the concept of natural health was still well outside the mainstream of people's consciousness. Nevertheless, I could see that demand was increasing and that there would soon be a general shortage in the supply of quality organic products. I knew instinctively that we were heading in the right direction, especially since some herbal, homeopathic, and spagyric products where already sold in small markets, as well as a few professional skin care products that were naturally made.-

While I was making plans for a new life and business abroad, a novelty called the SPA—and new expressions like "wellness" and "holistic lifestyle"—were existent but still laughed at, ridiculed, and overlooked by the medical, food, and cosmetic establishment. Some twenty to thirty years later, wellness and holistic health have rapidly gained mainstream recognition to become everyday slogans. I had been shyly using the word "wellness" way back in the late 1960s, and, over a span of twenty years, I saw wellness grow from being a little-known concept into what is now a trillion-dollar industry. The wellness industry will be the next big thing after the IT and biotech revolutions go through their down cycles.

In Europe, spas had a more clinical heritage dating back to ancient Greek and Roman traditions; they were being run by doctors and nurses without a lot of fun and joy. But across Asia and the United States, the spa took on a new genre and offered an assortment of health treatments, mostly consisting of pampering, massage, and exotic body and facial care.

The Mandara brand revolutionized Asian massage when it opened its first spa bungalows on Bali Beach. They offered a fusion of local Indonesian massage strokes along with essential oils and doses of exotic health rituals. The concept of pampering spa treatments was an overnight success and by the end of the 1980s, Mandara Spas had mushroomed worldwide. Today the Mandara Spa in Tokyo, Japan, is totally booked a month ahead. As a Spa brand, the company was sold successfully to a large cosmetic company and a famous cruise ship owner. There are sophisticated architecture and design driven spa companies all over the globe that compete vigorously with each other. Now they all look alike and every small hotel and resort is told by marketers that they need their own spa to attract guests. After twenty years of dramatic spa development, customers, owners, and therapists are becoming bored with all the same menus and all the fancy names and unmet promises.

The whole concept of the spa has become a tad boring and is in need of some refreshed, renewed direction. Asked by a big player in the luxury resort and spa industry, I started to develop the next generation of experiences for a saturated spa industry. By 2005, I was ready to start the difficult patent process for the "JK7 Spa-Sensator" and was ready to enter the world market in 2008. The step from invention to innovation was complete after many variations and changes, which ultimately offered a stunning, never-before-seen tool for the well-being market and community.

The spa would never have reached such enormous popularity if it didn't align with the culture of wellness and the traditions of holistic health, in which the whole is viewed as being more than the sum of its parts. Much like alchemy, spas are a popular, friendly alternative to the often cold and clinical setting of conventional Western medicine. The reason why holistic practice works is that the treatments first address the cause rather than the symptoms—instead of the conventional Western approach of concentrating and operating on separate body parts and organs where the problem or pain is pinpointed. Unfortunately, the new age seekers first sold the spelling of wholistic as "holistic," resulting in a mistaken idea that spas and wellness are in some way related to the "holy" industry of religions, hippies, and dreamers. I decided to stay completely clear of the pseudo wellness groups that lacked substance or health expertise and, consequently, had little staying power.

Once the decision was made to leave Germany, I had to find new land and a base to set up my laboratory for research and manufacturing products. Adopting Solomon's wisdom, I quickly ruled out Ireland as climatically unsuitable, the ultraright tobacco lobby in Virginia as unfriendly, Southern France as too expensive and unionized, and the Philippines as unstable. That left only New Zealand and Australia, and I immediately booked a flight to Auckland on the invitation of the NZ government. After they accepted my business plan, they offered me the use of some spacious land for thirty-three years—free of charge—to start my business. I was inclined to take the offer, but after testing the water and soil, I found that it was heavily polluted by herbicides, pesticides, insecticides, phosphates, and nitrates. That left me with only one other option on the table and I quickly headed to Australia where a German biodynamic farmer by the name of Alex Podolinski had offered to help after I had secured some land.

The final choice was the Adelaide Hills in South Australia, which were green in winter as in Europe, but extremely dry and hot in summer. A local business helped me to rush immigration approval for my family and business. The Ambassador of Australia in Germany helped me personally by swiftly fast-tracking all the paper work, and he warned me that if the Labor Party were to win the election with their candidate Bob Hawke, a former hard-line union leader, and then the government would be much less welcoming to business immigrants. His vision became true later, but luckily, we had our immigration approval before that time.

Alex Podolinski had worked with Rudolf Steiner's knowledge, and it seemed to me that the forces of attraction were at work and would deliver the right cooperation on the farming side. What I liked about Australia was that it was a new country with a culture of less than two hundred years. The "lucky country," as most Australians knew it, had a lot going for itself and offered many Europeans a fresh start and a new place they could call home. The painful downside was for the Aborigines, who lived there in freedom for forty thousand years before the British conquerors arrived with lots of prisoners in 1788. Later, when I started a project with my company to grow native plants and Noni trees on Aboriginal ground in the Northern Territory, I had a life changing experience with my youngest son Jonas. At the age of eighteen, he was overseeing this charitable project and others.

My family arrived in Adelaide in October 1983 bringing with us one container each of laboratory equipment, machinery, raw materials, herbs, essential oils, and soy whey. A second container was filled with various household goods and plenty of books, which enabled the new laboratory to begin small production immediately. As it turned out I was given two farms—one with a house for my family to live in, and the other to grow herbs, plants, and flowers for the new health product line. Any doubts about leaving Germany soon dissipated as my wife and children quickly adjusted to the open, casual lifestyle and beach culture. Fortunately, there was already a Steiner school set up in Mount Barker in the Adelaide Hills, and I was able to focus on getting the new business up and running without the worry of caring for my children's education.

The first company I set up in Adelaide was called Jurlina, which began selling a medium-priced range of products to America, Germany, and Canada. The early business was carried out in a delicate relationship with an older Australian couple. However, our business agreement abruptly ended when we felt cheated and demoralized by destructive, anonymous letters that had been typed on the business premises of our partners and sent to good business friends of ours in Europe and America. This was verified by a forensic specialist found in an ensuing court case. The result was that we lost our home, the shed we used for a laboratory and a great deal of production. Instead of making products, we were forced to defend our reputation to keep the business alive. Without a base to work from or land to plant much-needed herbs and plants, I could see that the business opportunity had eroded into a no-win, high-risk enterprise in a foreign county with no income or cash. This was a heart breaking time full of sorrow and pain, and was made worse by our partner's determination to throw us out of our newfound country and obliterate our hard-earned business and reputation.

Adding to my problems was a legal battle I was embroiled in—a copyright and royalties lawsuit in Germany involving natural color paints. The royalty should have given us some financial security during our start-up in Australia. As things began to tighten, I decided that I would hunker down in Australia to find solutions, and sent my wife and four children back to Germany to stay temporarily with Ulrike's family. Soon I was able to find a small house that I promptly moved into along with my laboratory—then an assortment of raw materials and some new natural products I was in the process of developing. The court settlement in Germany awarded us a lump sum and with it, our temporary survival in Australia was secured. In August 1985, we registered our new company, Jurlique. The name, a combination of my wife's and my Christian names, was an excellent idea of our friend Gabrielle. Sometimes a name can work wonders, and from the outset, Jurlique had a winning aura.

Suddenly the energy began to shift and the looming darkness turned into some sunshine. My financial situation suddenly shifted up a gear when my distribution contact in the United States offered to pay me eighty-six thousand dollars if I could supply a new range of products for an order that needed to arrive in the United States by June 1986—just a few months away. I quickly set about making spagyric extracts with our good German friends, Karin und Baldur, in their private kitchen. Other work involved mixing essential oils and concentrates and securing other raw materials for about twenty thousand natural cosmetic units—all of which had to be put into boxes and labeled later. Some packaging materials were imported from Europe and the rest were sourced in Australia. But we still had no manufacturing facilities in Australia after the grim separation from our partners.

I rented the operational site of my tofu-producing friends in Germany for three weeks, and hired their staff to manufacture the ordered products hygienically and professionally. I then flew fifty boxes, along with myself, to Germany. Having arrived there, I found that the raw materials and packaging materials were lost. They were located one week later in an airline shed in Canada. Customs problems with the German authorities and other obstacles forced me to start and finish the huge job in less than two weeks, against all odds. Like a slave driver, I pushed the staff and myself day and night to manufacture, fill, and pack about thirty different products using the same machinery I had bought years earlier when I helped to start Florin. Only two days before shipping the products to the United States, the Chernobyl nuclear disaster happened. Heavy radioactivity rained down over Southern Germany and it was impossible to go outside or even cross the road to get to the storing shed. Despite all these difficulties, I was still determined to get the shipment on its way.

The $86, 000 payment was waiting when I returned to Australia, and I sensed that the difficult beginning stage had been overcome. From our new friends Charlotte Schwenzner and Joy, a psychotherapist, I got a bridge finance for six weeks for all the raw materials, the cost of manufacturing and my trip. I proudly paid the money back six weeks later from the first proceeds from America. More important, though, was that this money secured an ongoing distributorship in the

United States with the Kitchener Family. The turnover in the first year reached $180,000 Australian dollars, and seventeen years later Jurlique sold products worth $50 million Australian dollars per year to twenty different countries. My company therefore belonged to the small 3 percent of start-up companies who financially survive the first seven years. Some have kindly told me that Jurlique was the success story of a mission impossible.

With the first major order was delivered, the cash enabled the operations to be based in a new place: an old cheese factory. In 1987, the first herbal seeds were planted by Ulrike in organically prepared fields, and we set about manufacturing the first batches of herbal, spagyric medicines. Within two years, the company had grown to ten employees and we had distribution representatives on three continents. Our reputation for producing the finest health-care products on earth resulted in Jurlique's enthusiastic reception at two of the biggest cosmetic and health-product trade fairs in Hong Kong and the United States. There we found distributors for Singapore, Hong Kong, Malaysia, Taiwan, and Japan. From that first order the Jurlique ledger went on to turn over one million dollars annually by the turn of the decade and arrival of the Roaring Eighties.

With a demand for more space exceeding our ability to supply, Jurlique was able to secure a loan of one million Australian dollars from the Commonwealth Development Bank (with the help of the visionary manager and our "Angel Mr. Smith," as I called him later). This enabled us to build a state-of-the-art health product factory at the foot of the Adelaide Hills in Mount Barker. Our usual National Australia house bank flatly refused the loan, and I am sure they later regretted missing out on one of the country's fastest growing businesses. Some of the better land in the country was selected for an organic herbal farm in the same area that exclusively grows organic herbs, plants, and flowers.

With the business getting into high gear and running smoothly, I turned my attention to building a double-dome ecological house for my family, along with an organic veggie garden watered from wells bored fifty meters deep. Ulrike had a background in horticulture, and looked after the farm and some bookkeeping for the company. I managed and looked after the rest—doing all the research, manufacturing, quality assurance and control, distribution, sales, marketing, human resources, advertising, overseas trade, communication, and all the public relations. Some of these skills I had to learn quickly on the job, and others I had already developed. Staff grew from one in 1986 to ten in 1988, fifty in 1991, and then about four hundred in 2002. Because of the fast expansion worldwide, revenues sometimes doubled from year to year. I had to rush and work hard to create enough reliable systems and procedures to run the company so that the manufacturing did not outstrip the organizational structure.

While life had taken a turn for the better, we were far away from the easy life. For the first three years, my family made ends meet on my basic wage of nineteen thousand dollars per year. Our prudence soon paid off rather handsomely, however, as we sold as many products as we could manufacture. Our laboratory was hard-pressed every day, distilling essences and spagyrically extracting natural nutrients for our exclusive range of skin and body care products. Most importantly though, the business operations brought in sufficient cash flow to move Jurlique slowly out of debt and into trading healthily in the black from 1992 onward.

In our second year together in Australia, my children and Ulrike spent their Christmas days filling bottles and sticking labels while I was making thirty-plus different products in bulk, and while we all picked and dried herbs from our farm. Today I can look back on those early years of establishing our company in the Adelaide hills as the happy days as we were indeed a happy family, inspired by our natural health mission and a bit of visible success. But there was also a lot of underlying fear that we would not make it financially after such a rocky start. A ten- to fifteen-hour workday—six to seven days a week—was the price I had to pay for our success. However, I wasn't complaining. Ulrike did the same with the kids, the house, and the herb farm. There was no time to be unhappy or negative. The price had to be paid later, however.

By 1991, Jurlique, with its brand new pharmaceutical premises, was the first new company in South Australia to be accredited with the prestigious Good Manufacturing Practice License (GMP) to manufacture herbal/pharmaceutical goods for international markets. This was no easy task to accomplish, as getting GMP approval stretched from the factory facilities to well trained staff, right through to the raw materials and the laboratory procedures, rules and regulations. If just one complaint of a bad bottle of product was traced back to the factory or to the skills of our laboratory and manufacturing staff, or even to faults in the new IT system, we would have failed to qualify and Jurlique would have lost its early reputation of truly having the purest health products on earth. We wanted the highest accreditation possible and we got it. We walked our talk, following the ancient alchemy adage: "As inside so outside, as outside so within."

Jurlique's Government Health Department accreditation was enhanced by my personal appearances on TV, favorable stories in magazines and newspapers and by our passionate customers. Our customers endorsed the brand's growing reputation and believed in us so much that we were viewed in Australia as a valuable company ripe for takeover. But while the big boys looked in from the outside, my focus remained on building up our goodwill and assets by trading more quality goods more profitably. The wellness industry was now expanding quickly worldwide, and from southern Australia, Jurlique had gained an inside poll position. The scene was set for some hard and fast trading to about twenty countries overseas, with a second head office in the U.S. city of Atlanta, Georgia. Having been laughed at and belittled by family members in Germany and elsewhere in the 1970s and 1980s, Jurlique was living proof that rigorous, pioneering work in a new area—and in a new country—could work out successfully.

Many tried to jump on the bandwagon and duplicate our

success, when it was seemingly safe to do so in our exploding industry. The competition thus grew strongly and I used every public appearance, seminar, and workshop to point out the substantial differences in what Jurlique was doing—it was organically and alchemically pure unlike some of our competitors. Many of them used chemical and artificial substances and substandard formulas for their health and beauty products, all the while making similar claims of purity. Our close friend Gabrielle Wagner coined the phrase "the otherness of Jurlique." With decades of experience behind her in the beauty industry in Australia and America, she helped us develop more professional and streamlined treatments for Jurlique in both the beauty therapist industry and in Jurlique's concept spa stores. Some twenty-two years later, Gabrielle continues to run a Jurlique branded store in Santa Fe, New Mexico.

CHAPTER 9

The Roaring Eighties

"If you really want success, embrace change now!" That was the mantra and battle cry for corporate America in the early 1980s, as the perception of getting "easy money" turned the financial systems upside-down. As I settled into my new country "down under," fully focused on manufacturing a new brand of organic health products for an eager market, those heady days of instant cash injections passed me by and appeared only as powerful illusions.

Dealing with change is never easy when you are starting up a new global business. The temptation of joining the club and getting quick cash or greedy financial partners can be extremely appealing as it's very easy to be captivated by fast-moving trends and "easy" finance schemes. But I was somehow protected and fortunate that in the midst of the hurly-burly excitement of the get rich quick propaganda, I had a down-to-earth understanding that one rash mistake can flip a fledgling company over and—before you even know it—your business can find itself running off the rails.

The early 1980s were bold, brazen days for doing business in Australia. The tall poppies of the Australian corporate world watched the excesses of the American junk bond era with envious fascination. This was an exciting time when business entrepreneurs set new benchmarks for daring, pretension, and living the lavish lifestyle. As is the tradition for Australian society, it takes about five to ten years for an American trend or fashion to be accepted and adapted into the country. This no longer applied in the 1990s, when junk bonds became normal. Now a new wave of hedge funds, futures, derivates, and other "safe products" drove Australian banks and businesses crazy with their unheard-of profits. It took until 2008 for every taxpayer on earth to pay the hefty price for this globalized, corporate, and personal greed.

When the junk money finally flooded in, it provided a tantalizing menu for big billionaire players like Alan Bond, the hero of Western Australia and the America's Cup-winning yachting tycoon. Bond spectacularly overplayed his corporate hand by spending other people's money so extravagantly that he ended up in prison in much the same way as a plethora of U.S. junk bond corporate raiders. One of these raiders was later involved in buying a stake in Jurlique. He was by then—in 2003—a transformed man. And then there was the famous case of Christopher Skase who, after building two outstanding and acclaimed Mirage resorts on the Gold Coast and Port Douglas, was hounded for tax evasion and other financial irregularities in several countries. He finally suffered the ignominy of being wheeled into a foreign court with oxygen tubes up his nostrils due to his rapidly deteriorating health. Despite escaping into the so-called safe haven of Mallorca, Spain, he was pestered day and night for years by the agents of the Australian tax office and police. This superbly scripted tragic comedy ended in his unfortunate death.

The natural order of maintaining balance was pushed to the limit by big spending corporate America during the hay days of junk bond fever—a ten-year period of excess that rivaled the freewheeling days of the Roaring Twenties—some sixty years earlier. By the time the shaken establishment made the belated evaluation that a change had to happen, a wake of corporate carnage was left behind, and poorer people were forced into cashing their nest egg savings. The sheer craziness of the time saw a famous Australian medical doctor open a private blood bank for people to store their own blood for recall when and if needed. Revenues from Doctor Eddleston's personalized blood storage house, financed by willing investors with ego-longevity at heart, went entirely into buying the glamorous Sydney Swans Australian Rules Football Club franchise. Some visible and impressive leftovers of that time were the property developments on the Hyman Island Resort and the former Bond House in Hong Kong.

But while most of the big high-yield bond hitters finally went out spectacularly—with a whole load of bad press and expensive litigation—most of corporate Australia just watched from a distance. They were bedazzled to see the institutional American financial system garner together its full force to push back the waves of bond money that were flooding the market place. Finally, when the financial institutions did execute their combined political, legal, and commercial clout, the contest, in boxing parlance, was a one-way "mismatch."

The banking fraternity dramatically knocked out the junk bond schemes with the States' chief prosecutor of the day, Mr. Rudy Giuliani, who was to become the flamboyant mayor of New York City. Former junk bond superstars suddenly became the villains and bad guys. They were paraded in handcuffs as corporate criminals that no one wanted to know. Yet despite the ruthlessness of the clampdown that included billions of dollars in fines and lengthy ten-year prison terms for the king pins, the idea of accessing easy-to-get financial start-up cash still captivated the hearts and minds of a new generation of capitalists. They thrust themselves into the fast lane with such enthusiasm and optimism that the cities of Las Vegas and Atlantic City were rebuilt in a few short years, turning what were once seedy gambling cities into glamorous resort hubs for pleasure seekers, families on holidays, and of course big fat cats and high rollers.

The arrival of the junk bonds saw the introduction of a bold new business philosophy. The bad old days of tough financing were declared dead and irrelevant. The new way forward was based on the appealing principal that you could get everything you wanted by simply saying yes to easy finance. Vast amounts of investors cashed the burgeoning get-rich-quick league, which naively wanted to believe that capital was the quick fix monetary medicine for all business needs. The mistaken belief at the time, however, was that skilled and talented people only needed start up cash to crash through to the next level of perceived prosperity. They had to learn the hard way that cash is only part of, and not the whole, of business success.

In Australia, bonds promised both cash and instant traction, and during the early 1980s getting cash loans were "easy meazy" as there were plenty of willing and eager investors to punt on new ventures. While the information age had yet to stamp itself on the corporate world there was compelling evidence that a technology revolution was just around the corner. For example, the arrival of the fax machine excited business executives as they imaged drawings and text down a telephone line. I had one of the first high-quality fax machines in my business in 1986, which saved me from daily drives to a telex office fifty kilometers away. In Australia in the early 1980s, few people were switched on to the potential of technology for rapid communication, and the concept of personal computers and electronic mail was still considered by most as being the geeky gadgetry of astronauts, bank chiefs, and military generals.

Nevertheless, despite the conservatism of corporate Australians reflected by their resistance to change, there was a genuine excitement and admiration for the daredevil bravado of the U.S. junk bond kings that went down punching hard at the traditional banking system. Just like public stocks, junk bonds went up and down according to a company's fortunes, which enforced the public view that stocks and bonds were validated chips for respectable, public gambling. Before the junk bond tycoons were reclassified as corporate raiders by the establishment, they were able to credibly explain to would-be investors that those who dare to win had the one-way ticket to a cashed-up financial heaven. Of course, some risks were involved; but they argued: "If your aren't prepared to risk everything, you won't be able to get everything that you want." This is not to mention the ideal of "greed is good!"—widely propagated by Hollywood and the American mass media.

The new society of the Americana rich in the early 1980s, which amassed billion dollar fortunes from financial start-up schemes, viewed easy money as "now power" and the best protection for an unknown future. Adding further to the appeal of instant cash was the philosophy that high-yield bonds were the lifelines for the next generation of corp-execs who were ready for takeoff. The problem was, though, that the rising stars of corporate America were left unserviced and were eventually abandoned by the legal system. Financial institutions poured billions and billions of dollars into Third World countries with the mistaken belief that a flooding of ready cash would somehow create a demand for more expensive made-in-America products like the petrol-guzzling Cadillac automobile.

Ironically, while loaning money to new, needy, less greedy businesses in the United States was deemed an unnecessary risk, much of the trillion dollars that went into South America and greater Asian countries as loans defaulted, and the terms for repayments had to be renegotiated. And while the banks were forced to lick their wounds, what happened domestically in the United States filtered through to corporate Australia. At first, the bond financiers exuded a zealous vibrancy, selling long-term fixed interest capital to hundreds of expanding companies. As the bond business soared, the banks faced a cash squeeze caused by a lack of demand for their less generous loan terms.

Fearing a forceful backlash from the banking institutions and traditional finance institutions, influential politicians and the financial media fingered the junk bond traders for irresponsibly manufacturing loads of "funny money." Being under attack the financial entrepreneurs went public—selling the idea that all new products and worthwhile ideas should be perceived as "junk"—thereby invalidating the traditionalist view of what capital really is, while giving credibility to the bond traders. Despite the rhetoric from banking institutions that purported to fully protect the system by viewing junk bonds as the enemy within, the renaissance of Las Vegas and Atlantic City was not only evidence of the value of those bonds as a financial start-up, but also provided the crowning glory for the junk bond easy money revolution.

Fueled with cash from junk bonds, investors swamped to the gambling hub of the Arizona desert. The golden city was redeveloped into a quality resort for family entertainment. Internationally renowned shows and attractions took center stage in all of the leading casino hotels every night of the week. Las Vegas was won back from the mobsters by the junk bond dealers who took money managers into the casinos and showed them that the business of gaming was not only legitimate, but that returns for investments were guaranteed. The gambling tables and machines were all geared to a law of statistics based on certain probabilities involving the number of users.

This sound business knowledge did not go unnoticed by Australia's media magnate at the time, Kerry Packer, who began moving investments away from his core television and magazine businesses into the new casinos being built in Melbourne and Sydney. As far as Kerry and his son James were concerned, the business odds of a casino were simple and transparent in that for every amount of money spent by the gamblers the casino gave back 90 percent and kept 10 percent of the revenues. This 10 percent enabled casinos to record millions of dollars of profit in a single night. History has recorded that the high-yield bond entrepreneurs not only rebuilt Las Vegas, but also gave gambling a whole new legitimacy for business-minded people. In 1988, Americans legally gambled $220 billion dollars, and more than half was spent in the 24/7 Vegas hotels. Junk bond investments—amounting to $2.2 billion dollars—not only enabled Las Vegas to become a major international city, but also resulted in the state of Nevada continuing its development at a record pace. It is still America's fastest growing state.

While Vegas bloomed with the junk bond cash revolution, the downside of excessive greed saw a ruthless overselling of finance that began to spread like a contagious disease. It eventually would have to be stopped. In the beginning of the

1980s, junk bond traders were generally known as responsible—and even enlightened—financial operators. But by the middle of the decade, the media and legal systems—led by Giuliani at the time, America's chief prosecutor—had transformed their reputations into being corporate raiders, driven by greed, and with no regard for the welfare of their stockholders and staff. The media eventually depicted these opportunists as the corporate gunslingers who plundered and corrupted; their motto, that winning was not only good but also godly.

Will the current trend, with trashed speculative mortgages and a complete financial dependency on China, trigger a similar, or perhaps an even worse scenario? We have not yet seen the end of the biggest financial crisis in history. We are facing globalized unemployment and debts in the trillions that could never be repaid by all the taxpayers together on earth. The once arrogant "free" markets and large companies are falling more and more under government control. Karl Marx would smile if he could. Endless greed is leading to complete control. George Orwell's vision in his masterpiece, *1984* (which was actually written in 1948!), is becoming true in a subtle but perfect way.

The former white knights—who heralded the advent of a new world of unlimited finance—preached that high-yield bonds were a savior for the stale corporatism that had squandered their shareholders' hard-earned savings on personal indulgences. The unsavory truth, as portrayed by the establishment to a sympathetic media, was that the corporate raiders had embarked on a policy of exporting America's lifestyle disease of lavishness to countries like South Africa and Australia. The tabloid press gleefully reported on the proliferating bond culture of CEO's who spent fortunes on easy transport such as private Lear Jet aircrafts or fancy helicopters. The junk bond traders and their associates were living the life of a privileged class of reborn kings, their churches supported by illegitimate wealth. According to the traders, their self-image as junk bond tycoons warranted them flying to London to buy ten thousand dollar hotel suites.

An incredulous public was informed that the bond traders' ravenous lust for acquisitions was matched only by their accumulation of all the luxuries life could offer—including boutique apartments, expensive art nouveau paintings, caviar from Russia, rare champagnes from France, luxurious race cars, hundred-million-dollar yachts, and illegally imported Cuban hand-rolled cigars. The men of the 1980s corpocracy rarely separated pleasure from business and enjoyed being seen with TV celebrities, rock stars, and movie legends. While fragile and vulnerable on the inside, these raiders craved legitimacy on a public playing field. They took every measure to grab the media limelight and found out quickly that the fastest way to be recognized was to spend big. They did so, to the delight of the ever-growing paparazzi, with unparalleled and unabashed extravagance. In Australia, at the height of the greedy 1980s, the male pack leaders of blokey utopia demonstrated their manliness by dumping their aging wives (despite expensive plastic surgery), and selecting much younger companions to be their privileged consorts. The new women signed the deal of their lifetimes—for all the money they could ever want

While Australia thrived on getting into the junk bond "revolution," the U.S. establishment, backed by traditional corporate America, finally screamed "enough" so loudly that something had to give. The first sign that the establishment was ready to go to war against the raiders and their bond culture occurred in 1985 when the Junk Bond Limitation Act was first disputed. An open war for control of money and spending was officially declared when the former New York mayor and 2008 presidential aspirant, Rudolph Giuliani, then the U.S. Attorney, launched an investigation into Drexel and other corporations fueled by "un-American funny money."

While the raiders sought safe havens, the establishment's crackdown on insider trading finally brought the junk bond kings to their knees. They chose to plea-bargain for reduced jail sentences and some hefty billion-dollar fines. To this day, insider trading, along with price fixing, remains one of the strangest crimes of capitalism and is extremely difficult to define. No government has been able to clearly articulate what inside trading means, as knowledge of the market place is the vital fuel for all stock exchanges, personal and company profits worldwide. It's a fact of life that Wall Street brokerages do all their number crunching based on reliable information. Likewise—in the shops and stores—what's the difference between setting a recommended retail price and encouraging a fixed price? While junk bonds ripped into the financial order in America, it wasn't long before the disruptions of "funny money" exploded with a big splash onto Australia.

During this period of extreme financial optimism and subsequent crashes, Jurlique, as a tiny wellness manufacturer, began to expand production in preparation for a major foray into the international arena. I had quickly realized that the Australian domestic demand would fall well short of our critical production targets. Australian buying behavior tended mostly to cheap prices and bargains and therefore low quality. But, between 1985 and 1999, a big change took place in the minds of customers based on quality education by Jurlique and other information. Now a market exists even in Australia, beyond the mediocre perception that "she'll be right mate." But until 1995, Jurlique was forced to focus overseas for its survival.

At the time, I resisted, quite rightfully, the advice to change the Jurlique's image as a brand of up-market quality into one that would accommodate more competitive price structures, and would therefore please everybody. The feeling that governed my heart and mind at the time was that the brand was the very soul of the company and that I could never allow Jurlique to become stifled by Australia's conservative restrictions and "meritocracy." Resisting the reductionism pressure, I persisted in freeing up the Jurlique brand so that it could travel around the world and both maintain and expand its early reputation for being "the purest health-care products on earth." In the years to come, as our yearly revenues jumped each year by millions of dollars, I was thankful that we never followed the advice to lower our standards or prices to gain a competitive edge. I opted for "wallet share," instead of the deadly profit-share mantra of the competition in heavily harvested mainstream markets, fueled by greedy players.

In many ways Australia was a hostile market that required loads of cash for a broad marketing campaign, and to make matters worse there were many companies ready and willing to copy or spoil any new health products that generated consumer appeal. Australian businesses have had a long habit of following blindly the mistaken view that the manipulated and uneducated "customer is king." I have always dismissed this notion as a pretension lacking factual evidence. Jurlique's ability to reap millions of dollars of profit years later was the result of what I called selling from the heart or "heart selling." The winning formula for success was not to follow the customers' demands, but rather to answer the question, "How can Jurlique love its customers and give them real value for money?—A good working product that is in fashion, ample education about values, and a greater ability to read and understand food and cosmetic ingredient labels to make educated and value-for-money decisions?" That style of questioning always separated us from the pack.

Information and education became our keys for expressing the unique Jurlique method of selling to and from the heart. We set about publishing our own newsletters, which explained the concept of holistic wellness as well as the quality of the Jurlique product range compared to that of its competitors. I also followed the ancient spagyric method by separating the good from the pack by learning to distinguish truth from fiction. This action was kind of like a cleansing process in the mind of the consumer, and afterward, I was able to make educated decisions through the new wisdom of spending only on precious and truly effective products and services.

We also spent many hours in customer workshops, but this time was well spent as was proven by the marked increases in sales. This successful period was in no small way the result of the synergy of attraction that resulted from heart-to-heart selling and buying. With this strategy, I marketed without money, ten years before I was included in Edward de Bono and John Lyon's book of the same title. *Marketing Without Money: How 20 Top Australian Entrepreneurs Crack Markets With Their Minds*, published in 2003, included stories of creative Australian business people.

Jurlique's market intelligence and intuition showed that if we continued to do things differently, our "otherness" would finally produce tangible results. What I wanted was for Jurlique to be different, which meant that it had to be courageous and stand as a taller poppy in the fields of the glossy main stream. Jurlique had to be careful everyday to avoid being cut down by those convinced that it is best to chop off the tall poppies—a popular Australian term and pastime. I didn't want Jurlique to stand out for the sake of being different, but I also wanted it to differentiate. Jurlique's success was never about fitting into the mainstream for survival. From the outset, the Jurlique brand was positioned to thrive outside of the square of the traditional health-care industry and the overrated luxury cosmetic industry. Success would not come through analytical brainstorming but by "heart storming!"

Through this radical differentiation in the marketplace, Jurlique was able to break the black and white, stereotypical thinking of crazy and expensive marketing, and instead adopt its own distinctive attraction that did not depend on being liked by expensive guru consultants from the outside. Ultimately, the company's success was never going to be achieved by lowering prices or by senseless advertising, but through a lateral and parallel thinking process and innovative marketing concepts that veered well away from rock hard, vertical, "logical" thinking. Heart-storming customers showed the way forward and we never looked back. Winning customers always takes time and effort. Getting new customers is the easy part, but holding on to them and maintaining them for life takes skill, commitment, and heart-to-heart communication. It also requires old-fashioned values like courage, faith, and honesty, and necessitates avoiding the neurotic mind trap with all its envy, greed, pride, and gluttony.

The fact that Jurlique was able to be recognized by a fan base of unpaid celebrities such as Michelle Pfeifer, Cate Blanchett, Pierce Brosnan, and Mel Gibson was not just because the product was spagyrically and organically the purest on the planet, but also because it was genuinely loved from the heart. Jay Leno didn't get a Jurlique facial on his highest rated TV show for his love of money. He did it, and with good humor, because in his heart he loved and understood Jurlique as being fun and different from all the other brands in the cosmetic establishment. This "difference" factor was reinforced when I was asked as an "outsider" to become a director on the board of the Australian Cosmetic Fragrance and Toilet Association. The previous president, Karen from Estée Lauder, told the puzzled CEOs who represented all the big name cosmetic giants at the time that the industry "needed new blood." She said that the creative ideas were coming from smart, small innovators and newcomers like Dr. Klein from Jurlique.

Though sometimes a part of the celebrity game in sports and fashion, I knowingly kept away from the limelight as I believed that the Jurlique range of products and services stood out without the need for publicity gimmicks. Laborers in China used our world famous and tremendously effective hand cream, and traded it on a flourishing black market. The Jurlique fan base had become a vibrant mix of real people: teenagers, mothers, grandmothers, journalists, sensualists, and sexualists, gays, lesbians, blacks, yellows, reds, whites, and greenies from all around the world. Those with heart all loved Jurlique for its exceptional purity. They made Jurlique a brand that was always in demand.

CHAPTER 10

HEART STORM: THE COURAGE TO BE DIFFERENT

As Jurlique grew holistically and financially, from being a baby business to an adult corporation, there were several crucial stages in the company's development. Gradually, new systems and better procedures were required so that more products could be better manufactured, marketed, and delivered to a waiting world in the most efficient way possible. Administering the business while at the same time being creative was never easy, but it was manageable because I was used to dealing with adversity in life. The ongoing challenge was always in maintaining sufficient substance—knowledge, skills, and cash—along with our "secret" spagyric technique and the practice of selling heart-to-heart.

I realized early that Jurlique would either grow with quality substance being its strength, or it would be exposed to the forces of mediocrity, as is the case with so many other brands. If the latter happened, it would result in a gradual decline that would eventually spiral into stages of stagnation. Highly paid consultants alerted me to a business phenomenon commonly known as the critical point of expanding too fast. Unfortunately, these experts got it wrong in their mistaken belief that things become problematic whenever a company grows faster than normal. What they should have been articulating was that it is dangerous for any company to expand quickly without substance or a fallback position. Necessary for healthy expansion is a proper planning structure contingent, along with a strong belief behind the brand and day-to-day leadership from the owners, the executive staff, and their competent team.

I didn't need to employ a team of consultants to know that Jurlique's substance and primary asset were in its brand, which had always reflected the quality of its all-natural, organically pure, exceptional herbal spagyric products. But what I needed to identify—and get a handle on—was how to improve the value of the brand's substance through better performance in research and development, sales and marketing, and operating systems. I also needed reliable staff and accountancy to show me the real picture on a daily basis so I could see early any developing patterns. This provided a reality check that affirmed there was in fact sufficient financial and human substance for quality, sustainable, faster expansion.

To keep an accurate track of all operations—farming, manufacturing, quality control, training, education, and distribution—I installed a new state-of-the-art computer system. Back in the early nineties, this was admired as a cutting edge technological innovation for a pharmaceutical-based company, along with the latest facsimile technology. The hard working genius of a Polish computer specialist helped translate my ideas and demands into "three dimension" computer language. Both inside the company and to the outside world, we had a system that kept up with fifteen years of computer advancements. Upgrades were done in-house and on a need to do basis. A one-hundred-plus page how-to manual capped off all the fundamentals needed for the practical side of running a quickly growing business.

Throughout my life as an alchemist, naturopath, inventor, innovator, and manufacturer of herbals, spagyric lotions, creams, and gels, I had always thrived on being creative. I kept my mind open to all rational influences and changes, including the metaphysical. Intuitively, I knew that a young growing company like Jurlique needed some strong gravity as too much looseness and creativity can easily slip into chaos, and that eventually sparks a cycle of decline.

My personality is that of a typical Libra, with lots of flexibility and air in my horoscope. The importance of fire and willpower is accentuated by the Leo ascendant. My whole astral life is about speed, fast movement, pointed, fast negotiations and quick, strong decision making. And it always seemed natural to go quickly and never slowly. But despite my appetite for speedy solutions, I was always able to get down from the clouds and stay grounded to earth. Even today,

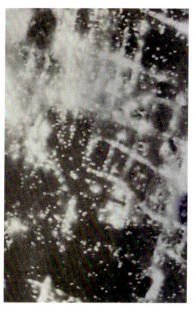

Allied Bomber over
Braunschweig 1944

Carpet bombing of
Braunschweig 1944

My Father, Gustav Klein, pilot in WWII

Jurgen and younger brother Harald 1949, title from local Newspaper
"Christmas for the poorest of the poorest"

Grandparents Gertrud and Heinrich
Fricke with Jurgen
and brother Harald

Mother Gerda with Jurgen
and Harald

Father Gustav with Jurgen and Harald

College Certificate, with Dr.H.J.Reimers (Director), 1964

Swimming club Delfin Salzgitter (Jurgen, 7th from left), 1959

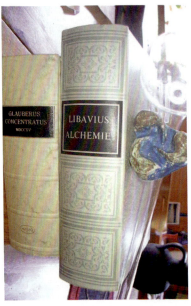

Two alchemy books, glass still, logo from clay for future company Jurlique 1984

Alchemy book, 1694, Libavius

Spagyric Book, 1715, Glauber

Alchemy symbols
(two-headed creatures)

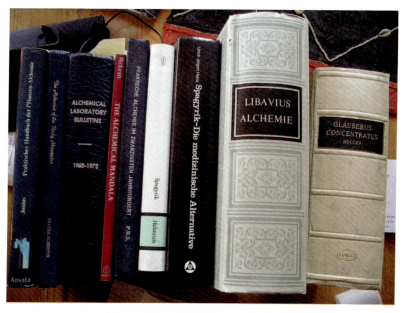

Group of Jurgen's Alchemy study books

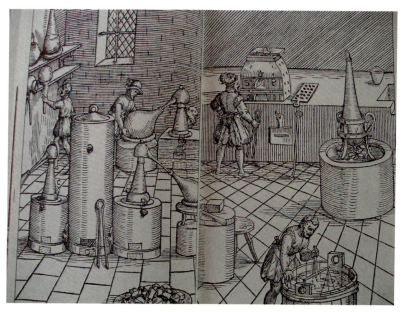

Alchemy Laboratory in 15th century

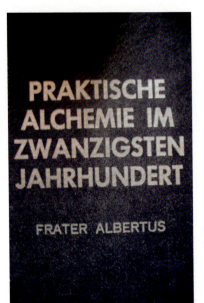

Book cover Frater Albertus,
Praktische Alchemie

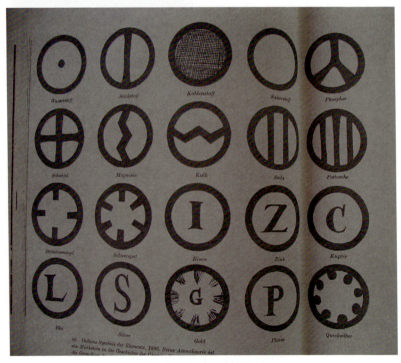

Chemical symbols in Middle Ages

Dr. Jurgen Klein on Jurlique herb farm, South Australia, 2000

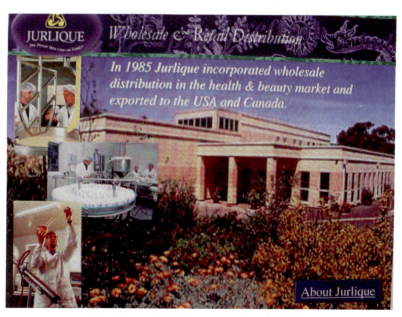
New Factory, Lab, Cream manufacturing, 1992

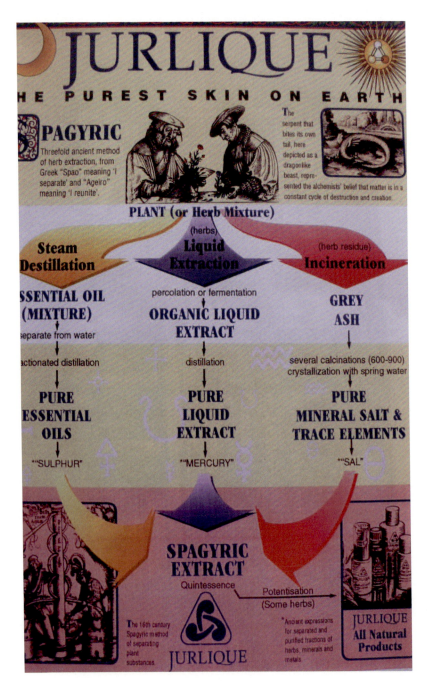

Spagyric Poster of herb extract production in 3 steps, 1985

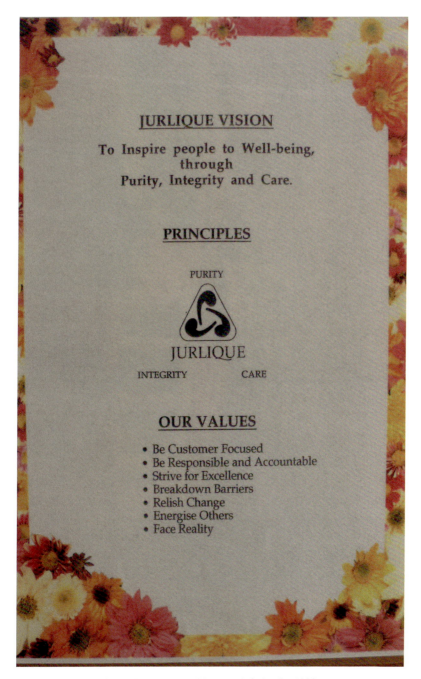

Principles, vision and logo with 3 distills, 1990

Frater Albertus and wife Emmy in Austrian mountains,
Alchemy class, 1979

Pierre Elliot and wife Vivian during class 1978 in N.Germany

P. Elliot class , lunch break

Helen Menock Class, Adelaide, 2000

Double-Hexadome house in construction

Left: Jurgen and his Double-Hexadome house, in construction, Adelaide Hills/ Herbfarm, 1989

Jurgen's Aboriginal Elder friend in Northern Territory, Australia, 1995

One of 6 Jurlique Hong Kong stores 2001 before opening

Jurlique store street poster

Jurgen Klein lecturing in a Hong Kong store with press and TV

JK with group of Magazine Editors on Herb farm, lecturing

Group photo herb farm

Thora and Jurgen Klein with journalist group in front of Adelaide store, 2003

CEO Jurgen Klein with Jurlique store staff in a Macao / China store, 2001

Jurgen Klein demo of products with VIPs in a Hong Kong concept store, 1998

Herb farm visitors

Sullivan Estate and Spa, Oahu, Hawaii.
Entrance to the JK7 Sensator treatment room

Fountains and watersteps

Yoga on Lanai above the famous North Shore of Hawaii

Sauna Room (Steam and, Infra-red and Finnish Saunas)

Volta Electric roof tiles and stand
(50 KW, 5 acre estate is self-sufficient in electricity)

Saltwater pool and main house, Sullivan Estate and Spa

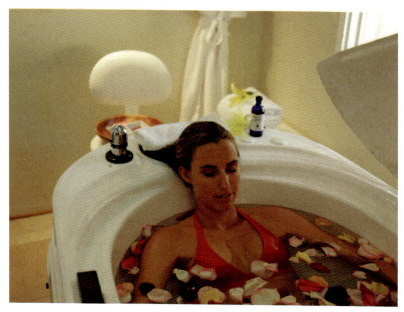

Hydrobath im JK7-Spa

Paradise Yoga

JK7-Sensator Room on Sullivan Estate and Spa in Hawaii

JK7-Spa Sensator software operation choices

Part of hardware for JK7-Spa Sensator

Color therapy with yellow in JK7 Sensator room

JK at 15,000 feet (5,000m) mountain pass after Shigatse (Road to Mt.Kailash)

JK with Blind school student practicing Chiropractic the Tibetan Way

JK at Shigatse farm (blind school), with sign of former Tibetan Herbal Medical school

JK at furnace/ herb-sacrifice place, Barkor Square, Lhasa temples

travel companions Claire and Kats

Claire, Kats and Californian Dr.Mark Lieberman in Shigatse
(eye-surgery as charity : operating many hundreds of people's eyes per months ,
saving them from turning blind)

Barkov Square column with prayer flags

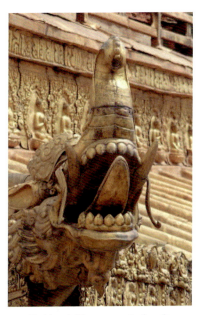

Golden Jokhang temple façade with dragon

Potala temple from Jokhang temple and golden statues

Flag with wheel and other symbol

Gyantse temple and Hill

Holy Hot spring bath place and Terdrom Nunnery, close to Lhasa

Stupa at Hot spring place

Horse with typical Tibetan colors and symbols

Hot spring place

The Potala in Lhasa

The Potala

Gyantse city

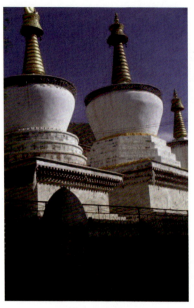
Stupas in Gyantse

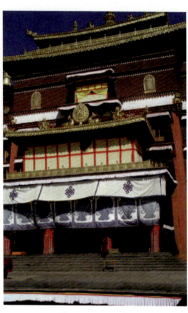
Gyantse temple

Tibetan symbol and money

Barkov Square Tuesday's,
herb fire/smoke sacrifice

Holy yak butter lamps

Cleaning oil lamps on Barkov square

Temple decoration

Sabriye Tenberken, Claire, Kats at school for blind children in Lhasa

Sabriye and Kats with Braille printer for 3 languages

Claire on blind school farm in Shigatse

Three blind children on Shigatse blind school farm

Blind boys with guitar singing, blind school Lhasa, rabbit class

Kats and prayer flag column at Barkor Square/Jokhang Temple

Boy and Baby in Barkor Square

Single prostrate

Prostrators at Jokhart temple

Modern monks with mobile phone in front of poster with admired European football players

Mud stamping workers in J. Temple

Yellow hat monks singing mantras

Teaching and controlling monk

Our SUV driver, teacher (observer for Chinese Government), Claire, Kats close to Shigatse

Last "non-5-star" accommodation night in Saga. (before returning to Lhasa)

Last "non-1-star" dinner near Saga

JK with dirt mask on mountain pass 15,000 feet (5,000m)

Yarlung Tsangpo River 12,000 feet high near Lhatse

Herd of wild yaks

Participants in the custom of throwing prayers printed on paper into the strong wind on high mountain passes (to calm the gods and secure a safe passage on those dangerous roads)

Prostrating monk and truck on dirt road in high mountains

Family of five high in the mountains

Nomad child in mountains on dirt road

Green valley, river, harvest, 12,000 feet high

Rugged high mountain country for cars and people

Shigatse, new part

Shigatse, old town

Our road through rough mountain ranges

Claire and part of new rail track from N.China to Lhasa, finished 2006, (now a 28-hour train ride)

Our truck with camping gear, cook, at 14,000 feet (4,500m high)

North to Northwest face Mt. Kailash

South face Mt.Kailash

North face Mt.Kailash at dawn

some of my family and friends have never really understood what my mission in life was. My intention was to be a provider of financial security to so many, while attempting to initiate change for a safer and happier living and ecologically sustainable environment.

One of the first lessons I learned about the health business was that no successful company could swim for long periods outside the mainstream. To survive and thrive, Jurlique had to find a strong niche where it could fit in best in a highly competitive main flow. Speed and the implementation of new ideas creates adversity and resistance, which sometimes can be hard to deal with—particularly since head to head competition is costly in money, time, and energy. Being impatient by nature, I was always learning fast while adapting under changing circumstances. As I saw it, cash without knowledge and skills was wasted potential, and knowledge without cash rarely can equip a company to take off and fly sustainably.

Within the space of two decades, Jurlique grew from being the baby of the Klein family into a confident corporate adult that naturally evolved and expanded with an abundance of substance. This was accomplished by sustainable trading that provided unique service, education, and quality products, and that did not allow investors and marketers to grab the hard-earned profit and then put the company into debt.

Jurlique opted on "wallet share" rather than market share. A never tiring and passionate Mark Wuttke, who later became CEO in our U.S. business to rescue the brand there under difficult circumstances, knew the pitfalls of illusory, consultant driven "marketing research." I believed in a proven Japanese method for introducing new products into a saturated market by first educating future customers while selling to them, and not by asking people for their opinion before the unknown product hit the market. When customers know and learn to like the product, they will open their wallet again and again. We had no need to worry about competitors and, instead, we could share the same customers with other companies and consumer products.

Nonetheless, we endured dangerous periods of low cash flow, staff issues, and disagreements during Jurlique's early stages of development; there matters required my intense care, courage, and attention. Some other successful entrepreneurs like me have built something substantial and sustainable from nothing, using only creativity and courage. The core belief that I instilled into the Jurlique management and sales/marketing team was that they should appeal to the customer's heart and avoid using what many professional marketers call "value for money."

By appealing to our customers' hearts and feelings, we got their attention without even being "pushy," and without spending a million dollars on some fancy advertising campaign. I have always believed that people communicate more effectively with their feelings than with their rational, money-oriented thoughts. This was the basic understanding that would make Jurlique stand out as different and independent from the likes of Chanel, Estée Lauder, Clarins, L'Oreal,

Shisedo, Delco, and Body Shop—as well as many others.

When King Solomon built his kingdom, he realized from the outset that he had little money, but he did have resources to trade. These resources, or products, included essential oils such as myrrh and frankincense and raisins—treasures that were perceived by his competition as having outstanding value that could not be matched. Similarly, without a million dollar advertising campaign, Jurlique had to bypass the usual hype by appealing directly to the customers' minds and hearts. To accomplish this, my first task was to establish a network of trainers and distributors who would not only follow their hearts, but who would share the company's passion to stamp the Jurlique brand onto a waiting world of baby boomers and nature-oriented people who, after two decades of excessive living and struggling, had decided to get their next kicks out of a healthy lifestyle.

Finally, a healthy life was no longer about pumping iron, running crazy marathons, or willing oneself harder and harder. Discovering health was a holistic experience, and it was this experience, of giving and receiving with a healthy mind, body, and open heart, that made Jurlique part of a new lifestyle. This would enable Jurlique to become a multimillion dollar industry. Inside the cultural movement of natural living was the purity of Jurlique products that appealed to customers' hearts and minds. I realized early that our products would need to be sold through their reputation by respectable, clean professionals who genuinely lived a lifestyle of wellness, and who truly believed in the values of being organic and "spagyric-minded." I also realized that Jurlique could never be a customized formula. I believed in and finally succeeded in "marketing without money," with Edward de Bono as my inspiration.

Another big asset Jurlique had was that as it grew stronger, it was regarded as a pioneering cultural hero of the natural health and environmental movement. Our core cause was that of wellness, health and longevity, and everyone who was associated with Jurlique—from the office clerk to the end user—were all convinced that the cultural movement toward a more natural and healthy lifestyle, and a cleaner environment, was no temporary fashion or fad. Rather, it was seen as a better way of living in truth. Jurlique needed wellness and wellness needed Jurlique. By putting the heart first Jurlique flowed, rather than struggled, with the fundamentals of efficiency and the desires of buyers. There was no need to brainwash customers with childish advertising.

During the later years of the 1980s, when Jurlique started to receive its first significant worldwide recognition, the technology and information age was still at the idea stage. Winning formulas were dependent on the reputation and the application of concepts. The experts used to tell me that competition was a necessary struggle for survival. But by using Solomon's secrets and trading from the heart, as well as de Bono's idea of "surpetition," we thrived as Jurlique grew up. We ignored direct and unfair competition and used only the synergy of wellness and selling heart-to-heart as vital connections. This holistic attitude and belief system was the foundational pillar. These core values manifested as business strategies and design concepts that put quality and great service first. "Quality, Integrity, and Care," and "The Purest Skincare on earth," became globally acknowledged as our main slogans, each enriched with the substance of our company and products.

As Jurlique expanded its markets and moved from the niche boutiques and health food shops into the top label department stores, the brand's products were perceived by customers, as well as astonished established cosmetic companies, as transcending normal competitive values. Jurlique integrated all the values of natural health with the popular wellness culture and helped to create a huge new sales and marketing base. Consequently, in a relatively short passage of time, Jurlique went from being just a health-care product line into a notable icon in an ocean of glossy and established cosmetic brands. By the time the 1990s arrived, Jurlique had reached a critical mass in its expansion and it became obvious that some adjustments would have to be made if the brand was to continue to grow globally.

The Jurlique strategy was to focus on quality of life in a polluted world, and a lifestyle of wellness—including a love for exercise, diet, naturally based health products, meditation, nature, family, and work. Living in a pure and simple way would always have a base appeal as life became more and more complex with each technological advance. More opportunities would become easily available with faster communication and the ever-increasing flood of information. But there would always be a basic, organic desire for the simple life and low-stress living. What people admired about the Jurlique concept was that, while it was associated with wellness, it never became superficial. It was not overly fashion oriented, and did not seek to artificially excite change in its customers. Wellness and Jurlique health products were perceived as an attractive alternative for those who sought escape from the dull, unsatisfying virtual realities of their compulsive everyday lives. Jurlique Day Spa stores in upscale shopping malls and on trendy streets were the perfect fit.

While it was not always easy to keep Jurlique in tune with synergies of the wellness lifestyle, I had the good fortune of encountering a philosophical master who made this more possible. He was a modern "mind alchemist" who taught people to see the world through its designs rather than relying on the hard logic of words. This man who pressed my thinking buttons was Dr. Edward de Bono, who managed to explain quite simply and brilliantly how the human brain functions. Through his new knowledge, he founded the concept of lateral, parallel, and nonlinear thinking. Basically, lateral thinking is the understanding that the brain acts as a system whereby information organizes itself into sequences. As Dr. de Bono explained, the human brain has evolved with a design mechanism that transforms all incoming information into an organization of patterns that can be used both creative and problem-solving processing. But, de Bono pointed out to me that the mind isn't just the thinking processor of pattern puzzles. According to de Bono, the human mind, when released of its inhibitions, can automatically produce an abundance of creativity and solutions for all the current problems in all areas of global life.

Because I'm a "spagyric scientist," lateral thinking did not come as a big shock to me. Indeed, all my inspirations in life had come solely from persistence and the lateral knowledge that holistic wellness and quality health products could be married together and turned into a thriving, global business. My understanding was that the difference between creative people and those who lack creativity was in their mental motivation and their heart's desires and true feelings. Applying this lateral understanding, I could perceive Jurlique's full substance. I realized that we had the soil to grow all the organic plants and herbs we needed. We had spagyric knowledge and a committed staff with proven systems to produce outstanding products of transformational substances. Customers were provided with the best products and services, not to just fit into the box of conventional consumerism, but to satisfy their hearts.

Lateral thinking encourages company leaders to break clear of "rock logic," and to instead use "water logic" to form more expansive patterns that spark insightful perceptions. I discovered that the "soft water approach" unlocked the doors of perception by moving the thinking process from the main track into a sidetrack so that the route back to the starting point becomes obvious in hindsight. This is a valuable marketing and surveying tool for evaluating a company's progress and considering its future potential. This technique is simple to do, as backtracking takes you to the beginning with a clear vision to be in the now.

Edward de Bono had another brilliant technique of moving patterns of creativity sideways across the mainstream outflow. The value of this side maneuver was that there was no direct resistance when one defined creative pattern was washed forward by the mainstream. "Sidetracking" with soft water logic removed the likelihood of coming into conflict with hard rock logical patterns of typical opposition. Linear thinking in science, politics, and business life finally leads to self-destruction.

The de Bono strategy of staying away from the mainstream until the appropriate time made a lot of sense for Jurlique. It was as an aspiring global player that was running head-on into a stream of fiercely competitive products. I had decided early on, in de Bono's language, to dance laterally—and so I headed to a side tributary of the mainstream competition to take some time, working quietly and nearly unnoticed behind the backs of the combat field of saturated markets and much larger competitors. I gave myself space to come up with a "soft water" creative strategy. In this safe zone of a gently flowing substream, I waited for solutions to rise up and allowed quality time for new ideas to form into patterns of creative intent. Here I prepared to reenter the mainstream well armed for synergetic attraction.

Taking time out in the lateral substream allowed "my fire" to keep glowing without burning too much creative energy. What became obvious was that for Jurlique to continue expanding with substance and value on the global stage, there would have to be lots of helpful synergy, and that would require making more connections. This could be done by establishing a stronger worldwide network of distributors. Additionally, customers who valued quality, service, and heart-to-heart selling over junk and quantity needed to be specially educated. Time out in the lateral thinking zone reinforced my perception that Jurlique's core appeal was in its lack of compromise. In the journey of the concept to the product to the market, there was always the utmost organic quality and spagyric approach. The work of the alchemist may be complex in our time, but when products and services transform customers' skepticism into the recognition of quality and pure goodness, all the complexity disappears like magic.

When it was time to return to the mainstream, my sales and marketing strategy was clear—Jurlique products would be known as being basically pure and simple, but complex enough to make them impossible to be copied. This offered two sides of the same coin without diluting the Jurlique brand and while maintaining a sense of mystery and uniqueness. Rarely do people appreciate absolutes, but everyone likes intrigue and enjoys the mystery of the unknown. As I saw it, most people liked to think like an inefficient combustion engine, using up all their energy just during the combustion process. The truth is that everyone gets the same light and hydrogen from the sun. People don't need to use a car with the horsepower of a chariot. Everything is provided for those who understand and use energy in the right way.

When de Bono brilliantly showed me that all conceptual understanding begins with defining what is lacking, I reached out to de Bono's tangible ideas to find out what Jurlique lacked. I wanted to achieve an optimum peak that could be maintained. What I found was that all the competition had to be replaced with "surpetition," whereby success comes from careful attention to integrated values that involve creativity with workable concepts. (Ironically, I had been doing this naively for twenty years, more or less consciously!) Taking it a step further, de Bono cited the Swiss watch industry, which recovered from years of decline as soon as the company marketers realized that they were not selling watches but jewelry and luxury. This analogy enabled me to see that the secret for Jurlique's success wasn't only in selling health products but also in offering to the world a brand of organic purity that spoke of a holistic lifestyle, longevity, health, and well-being. Jurlique appealed directly to the heart. I learned that it was not based only in the conventional and highly competitive cosmetic market, but instead was offering value in the form of environmentally responsible health and well-being products.

The Jurlique "heart" model for customer identification and attraction was simply to communicate, but it created an extraordinary reaction. The heart feeling is far more satisfying and wiser to behold than only abstract logical thinking, because everyone uses their heart spontaneously—first to form feelings that reflect the condition of the mind, and subsequently to spark behavioral tendencies such as selecting and buying. By addressing the heart's resistance, all doubt is dissolved, along with confusion and fear. At the same time, this process provides clarity of genuine feelings, thoughts, and action. Consequently, customers feel safe and confident in making sound purchasing decisions. An old Taoist book, *Balance and Harmony*, describes even in its title this lateral approach.

Once a pattern of the heart feeling exists, it is very hard to cut across it to establish any other pattern of resistance through logical thought. At the same time, circularity can be established which causes future emerging patterns to lead back to the heart. Triggering the heart sets off emotional synergy and clarity that connects heart-to-heart, and that, in this case, brings about images and associations of wellness and of the Jurlique brand.

What de Bono taught me, which I applied directly to Jurlique branding, was that by going directly to the heart, stubborn "hard rock" resistance is removed. By going directly to the heart, Jurlique customers could see, trust, and perceive something different from what another might see outside the dimension of the heart. This process cannot be cheaply imitated or forced on people by smart marketers and mass-market brands.

As I wrote in my early notes in life, which plotted a course for the future substance and sustainability of Jurlique, I realized that everyone is born on earth and will die here in a brief period. Only while we are living can we either make the world a better (or worse) place in which to live. Unfortunately for humanity, in the first decade of the twenty-first century, the human species is poisoning the air and water, while also wrecking earth's natural bounty and hard-earned savings by reckless bankers and investors. Generations will suffer the consequences of our selfish excess and stupidity in exploiting earth and society's delicate balance. Excess production of carbon dioxide, and even worse pollution, are not the only reason for global warming. The truth is that human beings could very well erode themselves from this planet by their excess of distorted logical and linear thinking. Relating to the world this way is responsible for deadly actions that are based solely on ego protection, and that are soaked in the poisons of greed, envy, hate, blame, and judgment.

As I jotted down my hopes that Jurlique would be remembered as a company that did good and not bad, I glanced over the trade revenue figures that showed in the first five years, from 1985–1990, sales had accumulated from $86,000 to $5 million. Those figures would continue to grow to the extent that by 2002, the annual net profit of Jurlique would be around $20 million, with yearly sales over $70 million and a net profit of over 30 percent.

I asked myself, why do some companies succeed while so many others fail? Certainly, much evidence suggests that rich parents teach their children how to be and stay rich, and conversely, poor parents teach their kids how to stay poor, as portrayed in Robert Kiyosaki's book, *Rich Dad Poor Dad*. But for me, it was the reverse situation; I could remember that, as a boy of barely eight years of age, I had a burning desire not to be poor like my family or war-torn like my father, who died at the age of fifty-eight.

My understanding, as an alchemist thinker, is that all material substances, including us human beings with bodies, minds, and spirits, can be transformed into something better. And while the will to succeed is a very powerful tool to carry in life, I very much doubt whether Jurlique would have been able to grow so strongly without the knowledge of Solomon's secrets, or without our own unique secret of triggering emotional synergy through "heart storming." I went into business believing that a company can't spend what it doesn't have, and that every transaction should accumulate more capital for new investments and expansion.

I also believed that a company should be debt-free to safeguard its future and have passionate staff, stakeholders, and owners. With the turbulent 1980s having gone by, Jurlique was in good shape. As the worldwide wellness industry entered into the mainstream with a big splash of high expectations, Jurlique had the substance needed to really make a difference.

CHAPTER 11

Full-Throttle Living

The three years leading up to the 2000 Sydney Olympic Games were a period of exceptional growth for Jurlique. The company had grown into becoming a wellness icon, and I was seen as some sort of a reluctant hero or guru of the natural health industry.

In the early nineties, I opened full service day spas, with company-owned retail shops, long before brands like Aveda, Clarins, Origin, Shishedo, and L'Occitane had even contemplated doing so. Jurlique developed new systems for spa retail that included excellent facial and body services in aesthetic treatment rooms. We set up model retail stores in prominent inner city locations and shopping centers in Australia and the United States, and a few years later, in Taiwan, Hong Kong, Malaysia, Japan, China, and Korea. I invested in role model day spas for our customer training courses, health and beauty services and general sales. The quality level of these spa stores allowed easier access to the services offered in brand-controlled areas of up-market department stores and airport duty-free shops. Over a span of just five years, Jurlique day spas had mushroomed around Asia and the United States, and the concept was now being copied by many cosmetic brands.

Jurlique had aligned itself to the booming resort and hotel spa industry, providing natural products that matched the high quality service ethic that was exuded by the better spas. Jurlique was seen as a fresh breeze, adding pure organic products, treatments, and systems to quality spa outlets. In many ways, there was a correlation between the growth of Jurlique and the speed at which the perception of the spa and wellness industry moved from being "niche-fringe-independent" to "health-quality-driven." Spas were late to arrive in Australia, and, as in New Zealand, the local population was slow to catch on to a life-changing industry and a lifestyle that had grown enormously. The hotel industry benefited tremendously from adding the value of spa wellness to their luxurious five-star hotels and resorts. The beauty and day spa industry had to first overcome the image left by the 1970s and 1980s, which saw body shops being more massage-parlor oriented (often with a sexual connotation) than havens for health and beauty.

Spas created a new clean image, with flow and style. Today, "destination" and "medical" spas exist where the rich and famous can stay overnight. And as long as one has cash or a credit card that hasn't been maxed out, the spa is open to them. Anyone can become an overnight celebrity by simply checking into a destination spa and mingling with celebrities, especially in Asia and the United States.

The fact that the spa industry rivaled new technologies and the worldwide web, along with biotech, as the world's fastest-growing industry at the end of the twentieth century, is an indication of how far the spa and attached industries have come in the last twenty years. For certain, it will overtake the sales and profit of the IT industry, and will again transform itself into becoming the next hardware for the wellness software. The spa has evolved in Europe from being a clinical enterprise into a fashionable culture, and today offers much more than just body scrubs and aromatherapeutic massage with essential oils. The spa industry fits nicely with all alternative natural health-care treatments such as body therapies, iridology eye analysis, Chinese acupuncture, herbology, naturopathy, homeopathy, and vibrational energy analytics. The treatments offered by quality hotel spas are still oriented around pampering oneself, but the modern spa menus take on treatments designed to both relax the body and mind as well as to unearth subliminal negative edges that affect well-being.

Like alternative and complementary natural medicine, the spa and wellness industry was initially branded as quackery. But all snickering and derisory comments quickly dissipated when spas went up-market into the five-star hotel and resort brands and the luxury cruise liners. Hoteliers embraced spas as a must-have addition and imagined them as cash cow facilities that could produce more revenue than their restaurants and bars combined. Consequently, it didn't take the cash-conscious hotels very long to realize that if they were to charge $20 for a beach massage, they could upgrade that same massage into a $150 service inside the spa, especially in low wage Asian countries. Smart hoteliers were quick to figure out that the number of "heads on beds" could be converted to the number of "bodies in spa" for big profits. And unlike fitness centers and exercise rooms, the spa comes complete with a full menu of prices just like a restaurant.

A well-run spa can be a main revenue earner for any hotel, especially during the low season when heads on beds tend to drop off substantially. Just as there are empty gyms, fitness centers, saunas, and swimming pools in hotels all around the world, the hotel and resort spas need to attract customers. Today's spa enthusiasts want to go beyond pampering and massage to the next level of spa wellness. They want to enjoy a new spa experience. I have been a pioneer of spa development for thirty years, and I know that the time is right for the next new spa sensation. Over the last seven years, I have developed the JK7-Spa Sensator, which synergizes natural therapy methods to the next level of spa wellness and longevity. It is fun and entertaining, while also providing therapeutic relief for stress, depression, fear, and the unwanted psychosomatic consequences of these mental states.

The crowning glory for Jurlique came in 2000 when the company became an official business participant of the Olympic Games Committee, and one of the sponsors of the world's biggest sporting event, seen on television in every country. We gave away our expensive tickets to the Games to selected staff, volunteers, and business people who had been involved with the success of Jurlique, which was doubling its sales and revenues every one or two years. There was no question that Jurlique was one of Australia's new, big success stories and after Kerry and James Packer worked out a deal to buy Jurlique, the press had a great time writing that I had arrived in the top 150 club of Australia's richest people. This was not the factual truth, since the money from the sale of Jurlique was stretched over a period of five years. Many negotiations took place during that time, and it was not always comfortable.

During the 1990s, Jurlique grew from being niche to having a place in boutiques and fashionable stores alongside the likes of Chanel, Dior, and Estée Lauder. The Olympic Games were viewed as a chance for Australian society to be seen and heard, just as at the famous annual Melbourne Cup horse race meeting. I was determined that Jurlique's sponsorship of day spa services, used by two thousand Olympic athletes, would have a practical purpose and would reflect core wellness values. Throughout the Olympics, Jurlique set up a spa with nine treatment rooms in the athletes' village compound, so that the Olympic participants could receive a full array of massage treatments along with our special Jurlique facials. Our expert therapists were invited from all over the world, along with fifty volunteer therapists from Australia who applied various herbal remedies and treatments for muscle aches, tears, and stresses.

At any one time, fifteen trained Jurlique therapists were

on site. They worked for sixteen hours a day and catered to Olympic athletes' needs for five weeks. The Jurlique spas for the Sydney 2000 Games were a huge success. Unfortunately, since that time, all the Olympic sponsorships have been taken out of reach for young companies like Jurlique. Instead, millions of dollars are paid to the International Olympic Committee from large companies like Unilever. But it was Jurlique who was the pioneer for this service during the 2000 Sydney Olympics. Now even Olympians needed a professional spa, not only hotels and resorts.

When my accountant, Mark, advised me during the track and field finals that five million dollars had been set aside in a separate account—from a small percentage of accumulating profits and bank interest over a five-year period—I was pleasantly surprised that that had been possible, and that Jurlique had developed such a strong leading edge in marketing and distribution. Our "heart storming" approach had been an extremely profitable strategy, but its primary function was to elevate Jurlique products in people's minds as not only natural and quality based but also as a status symbol for those who chose wellness as a lifestyle. It seemed to me that it was only natural that once Jurlique got into the winner's circle as a champion of natural health, monetary success would follow. In the rat race and grind of the everyday work mill, I had forgotten my own personal wealth. I had funneled all profits in the first fifteen years back into the business, and my family refrained from taking dividends and high salaries.

Sitting with the VIP sponsors at the main Olympic arena

while watching the cream of the crop of the world's athletes hold their gold medals in the air, the question arose in my mind, and not for the first time, "When would enough be enough?" I recalled that, in the wisdom of old and new masters, money wasn't the root of all evil. Rather, the attachment to money and the lack of it causes all dissatisfaction, greed, envy, brutality, crime, and worry. Nearly all people worry either about losing their wealth or about never making enough money. Both types act neurotically and never live in the refuge of present time where worries, guilt, and fears do not exist.

It took me fifteen careful years to put aside five million dollars in personal assets as a nest egg and a guarantee of financial independence for my family. But it was far more important that during almost two decades Jurlique had been a lifeline for hundreds of employees and stakeholders, and had become a leading source for the wellness industry. The charitable Klein Foundation was also carrying out valuable research with natural products, offering new hope for diseases such as AIDS, cancer, diabetes, and numerous allergies. They were also providing alternative therapies for addictions. I made a point to ensure that a significant percentage of Jurlique's net profits went into the Klein Foundation, which made certain that there was always sufficient money for new and genuine research with three universities in Sydney and Adelaide. That research is still going on and has reached its peak in 2007 and 2008.

While the money was flowing in, I had little desire to move

away from the simple lifestyle that had kept me content. Visiting VIPs from all over the world that came to the Jurlique factory and the herbal fields were often a little shocked when they saw me get out of my trusty Ford, Holden, or Subaru. I finally did accede to my executives' request and upgraded my transport to reflect the company's wealth status with the purchase of a new 4WD Toyota SUV. Perhaps it was Solomon's wisdom—or the sages' warnings—about attachments, but I never did enjoy the custom of showing off wealth and my holistic belief system insisted that I walk the talk of wellness. I had observed so many times where excess and extravagance manifested as disease. In all my research as a healer and alchemist I had seen so many examples of people dying prematurely, surrounded by their wealth.

The Australian male millionaires and some of their "ankle biting" second and third tiers liked to indulge in buying expensive "big boy" toys and partying with the guys. The trouble was that the big boys, like media magnate Kerry Packer—whose companies PBL and Consolidated Press, along with U.S. company connections who would eventually buy *into* Jurlique, and evaluated it at $146 million dollars—did not have the full physical armor to ward off the diseases caused by excess. Kerry Packer and his mates all liked to smoke, drink, and enjoy life's pleasures. The reason why Kerry's bright flame burned out in his sixties was that his mind could not live in moderation. He had no belief system other than to "crash through, or crash."

By the time I had gotten to know Kerry as a friendly associate with great humor, he had physically passed beyond the point of no return, which made me very sad. His kidneys were lost and his love for nicotine appeared to have reached the advanced addiction stage. Kerry Packer was like the big stars in the universe that burned bright for a brief life before going out as a supernova. When he reached his final days of living, it was reported in the daily newspapers that he told his staff to fire up his private jet plane for one last flight. He then headed off to Argentina to watch a polo game, accompanied by his son James who had become slim, health-conscious and a sincere philosophical truth seeker. James, who I have always liked, convinced his famous dad to buy Jurlique and participate in the ever-growing health and wellness market.

There are many who will say that our time on earth is very short—so why the concern for maintaining a wellness lifestyle? That may have been the viewpoint of Kerry Packer, who was adamant that there was nothing more after death and that life was about getting what you want. My reply to him, which hasn't changed much over the years, was that life wasn't a matter of how *long* one lived but of *how* one lived and contributed to humanity and the planet. My view is that living with a modest natural health and well-being approach soon becomes a routine—and a fun one. It is also beneficial as old age sets in.

Is there anything more important than having fun, financial independence, good health and a healthy sex life even as you're approaching seventy-five years and far beyond? By today's conventional medical standards, this is regarded as being nearly impossible. Men die earlier than women of the same age do, and are being confined to misery and sickness through weak hearts, as well as prostate problems, Alzheimer's, and Parkinson's. This decline is generally set in motion when men lose their jobs or retire, or when they have no other purpose in life than working for money's sake. It is my observation that healthy senior men are fast becoming an endangered species, and are suffering from a lemming-like, self-destructive ailment. Longevity seems to be mostly achieved and practiced by women of our time. They simply survive men, even in spite of the harder lives they may have lived.

My conversations with Kerry Packer were usually brief, as he was even more impatient than I am. I always had the feeling that Kerry would like to find something more than his self-professed fatal determinism. His larger-than-life approach was all about pushing and shoving, right up to the final curtain fall. But with his son, James, who loved the Jurlique brand and philosophy, I had an unexpected ally who had a sound understanding of natural health, meditation, and inner development. James not only followed the wellness path, but he also exuded a healthy persona at that time. He often said that being healthy was not just about being physically healthy—but also about looking good. He agreed with the Chinese rationale that it was the outside face that determined the inside state of being. For example, if a house were dismantled, brick by brick, it would no longer be a house but only brick and joinery. A house is perceived by how it looks and functions.

James and I often discussed the Jurlique philosophy and marketing strategy of communicating "heart-to-heart," which not only increased sales but also brought the body, mind, and state of being into one holistic interdependent life entity. James liked the holistic approach to life and agreed that the truth of the heart was a very powerful motivator. I explained to both Kerry and James that while we would never be able to reach an absolute truth, we could journey together in that direction.

During my conversations with James we touched upon the media and marketing, and how the culture in the financial cultures of the 1990s had become a powerful mechanism for changing values. We also discussed how, not long ago, non-smokers had to apologize for not being part of the smoking culture. It was once considered cool to smoke. Today, much to the consternation of smokers like Kerry Packer who was then fighting a dying cause, it is most often the smokers who are in retreat and apologizing (although Central Europe and China are slow to catch on).

At the same time, the growing culture of concern for the environment and ecological values showed how a popular cultural movement could express a powerful opinion and compel others to change social values. Politicians are a reactive species in that they always go along with the mood for fear of losing votes. My view, coming from a country that had lost its heart and soul in the biggest world wars, was that cultures based on hostility and warlike values are the continuing plague of humanity. These cultures have been responsible for the aggression, prejudice, and persecution that has arisen in the past and that continues today.

The truths learned from the approach of heart storming at Jurlique—while never unraveling any absolutes—had the wonderful effect of creating networks with synergetic harmony. I believe this protected the company from slipping into complacency or arrogance. Sometimes heart storming would require going back to undo certain compulsive and outdated practices to move forward. Quite often, the pieces can't be put together in a heartfelt way until they are free from their old configuration. I told Kerry and James that the core of Jurlique was about openness, otherness, and new ideas expressed through the feelings of the heart in a new, lateral way. The failure of many businesses, I further explained, was in the replacement of one rigid, retarded system by another rigid system. These systems divided people rather than meeting their needs of harmony between hearts, minds, and bodies.

When you reach a certain level of success, when your heart tells you that a cycle in life has run its full course, a state of emptiness along with a certain satisfaction is achieved. For me, this was the sad but realistic realization that this time had arrived. I saw that something of great value that I had created and nurtured for two decades now needed to be handed over and left to bloom and transform in a different way. But I had to accept that everything I had worked for could be destroyed. Nothing lasts forever. I had given Jurlique strong roots and a guiding heart, but now the time had come for me to let Jurlique simply flower without my future involvement.

On the one hand, my linear thought process was asking, "When is enough enough? Or should I continue?" And yet, on the other hand, through soft water logic, I could see other, bigger patterns emerging inside my heart and mind that needed freedom from my past; they were ready to bloom. What I had no knowledge of, however, were the bumps in life that lay ahead, and the tornado that was building and about to jolt me out of the fast lane and into a new period of awakening. I had never been able, in the past twenty-plus years, to really enjoy what I was doing. It was all duty—providing, inventing, innovating, educating, selling, and marketing—and the duty was accompanied by a lot of worry and fear. I had adapted to this way of life, and I perceived it as normal—my family situation included. I seemed to run away from myself, but my suffering ego always accompanied me, like a shadow.

After the Olympics, when all the cheering had subsided, my life became a nightmare. I flew three times a year literally around the planet, making busy side trips in Australia and short trips to Asia. I spent my spare time lecturing and coaching high-powered people and elite executives about healthy ways of staying alive and fit, so they could enjoy all their profits along with their big boy toys, and maybe develop a bit more care for the have-nots. I also spent a great deal of time in workshops and seminars with staff and customers worldwide. And I always spent a few hours a week swimming, exercising in gyms, and playing friendly tennis games on our own tennis court.

I easily could have become a kind of "Bill Gates of Wellness" or Jurlique the "Apple of Well-being." Book publishers invited me to write the next big bestseller. One publisher in particular wanted me to write a book entitled, *How to Become a Millionaire in the Trillion Dollar Wellness Industry*. I was constantly being asked for my opinion in the print and television media about the latest health food, cosmetic, and well-being craze. It seemed that the media was always demanding to know "what's next?" after my success with wellness. I had become thoroughly enmeshed into a full-throttle lifestyle, and, heading toward my sixtieth birthday, I was running and thinking faster than I had when I was thirty five. Staying healthy isn't hard when you know what to do, and fortunately, because of all those years of research and business in health and well-being, along with the knowledge I had acquired, it wasn't terribly difficult for me to walk the talk of wellness. The problem wasn't my health. The truth was that I had become so busy that I had no time to live, and I spent too little time with my family and friends.

My close Chinese friend and Chinese Doctor, Weibei Chen, was delighted to tell me that I was born in the year of Monkey with the element of wood. The monkey is known as the smartest animal on earth that can never keep still and do nothing. Weibei didn't have to be too clever, though, to observe that by nature I am a thinker and doer, and sometimes even a smart diplomat and something of actor on stage, born to delight people. But as I looked around and saw all the doers hanging on to their businesses until the last days of their lives, I had to ask myself again, "What next? When is enough enough?" Surely, success presents the opportunity for transformation. Isn't life supposed to be about change? Why hold on, when letting go will be so much better? Not letting go closes the doors that allow other opportunities to enter. I was desperate to let that opening happen.

I found myself being sucked into a celebrity lifestyle that went against my true nature. Being a showman in the media didn't rest easy with my inner being, although when the monkey in me does come out, I can be the showman, guru, and seducer. It seemed to me that my ego was growing—not quite out of control—but was moving in that direction. And if I was ever going to make the move to release myself from what I had created, then that time was now. Helen Menock, a tough American psychotherapist, gave me the last necessary kick by teaching me how to *stop*. The stop sign in traffic means, "Stop Now," or you risk a bad crash and fines. *Stop* means, "Never repeat the past again; it's over forever." Thank you, Helen. I am so grateful to have been accompanied by you through excruciating pain to transform my suffering, sorrow, and neurotic behavior. Helen also taught me how to "escape the Dragon's Pool," and she made me aware of what was required to deal with the "Tiger's Lair," a challenging ancient Taoist image.

I could see Kerry Packer sadly and slowly dying, with

his company directors carrying his coffin to his grave. The other Australian media magnate, Rupert Murdoch, delved into Chinese remedies to extend his longevity on earth, and to build up his immortal status with the encouragement of his new and much younger Chinese wife and their young child. But where did all this leave me? If my transformation were complete in becoming a simple philosopher or consultant, then I could continue in a passive role with Jurlique for the next decade or more. But what if I wanted to go the whole way into the "pathless land" in life, and understand the deeper meanings of who I am and why I am here? If I were truly going to explore the nature of being human, then I would have to fully stop compulsive linear thinking and behavior, and make some unpleasant decisions.

There was no doubt that Jurlique could survive and thrive without my involvement—if the new people listened and understood the risk of Jurlique becoming a small fish in a big pond, filled with stronger players. If I were to let go, there had to be someone else, or better yet, a strong, passionate group of people, who could take hold of the reigns. But would my attachment to the company I founded be too much to give up? To answer this big question, I alchemically had to work spagyrically and laterally on my biased thoughts and feelings. After some unexpected, stormy events, I carefully weighed all the options. Clearly visualizing the alternatives, the solution came crashing down to one singularity of nonaction: the time had come for sweet surrender.

CHAPTER 12

Sale of the Century

When I first met Kerry Packer, he was the reigning king of Australian women's magazines and the owner of GTV Channel 9—the country's highest-rated public broadcasting network. Aside from motivating his TV news team, Kerry Packer influenced politicians of all persuasions and became a major stakeholder in both the Melbourne and Sydney city casinos. Beyond being a media magnate, his main claim to fame was that he started World Series Cricket and revolutionized one of the world's most traditional sports. Cricket had been basically one long, five-day test match. Packer renovated it as a bat-and-ball slugfest called one-day cricket. I admired Kerry Packer for the way he seemed to alchemically transform a boring game into an exciting sport.

Kerry Packer was reported to be an old-style Australian cobber who enjoyed having fun, drinking beer, smoking cigarettes, and playing cards with his mates. He didn't enjoy being on the periphery of life. His style was up front, brazen—he always cut to the chase. Packer also liked the concept of deliberately running company business on the edge and to the brink, just as in a game of cards. Gambling was one of his life's passions. Kerry saw no reason to have a prudent reserve of cash, which was Solomon's wisdom that I instilled as the financial core of Jurlique's healthy trading system.

Before I first met with Kerry, I had discussed the operations of Jurlique with his son James and his executives. James was a fine looking, heavily built young man who inherited his father's business physique but who didn't smoke or drink alcohol at the time of our first meeting. James told me that he enjoyed keeping himself in good shape. He was a genuine person who loved talking about natural health care and metaphysics. When it got to the subject of Jurlique's trading and revenues, James and his executives were more than a little surprised to learn that the company kept several millions of dollars in cash and credit reserves. So when James first introduced me to Kerry, he promptly told his father that Jurlique wasn't just a good buy based on potential growth expectations, but also because the company had already established millions of dollars in cash reserves.

"What?" Kerry roared aloud. "What's this about then? You're telling me that Jurlique keeps millions of dollars as a cash reserve. Why's that?" I explained that having cash was a healthy way for the company to operate without any problems of cash flow and without becoming a victim of any bank. Kerry lit up a cigarette and said something like, "Is that so, ah hah, we'll have to see about that."

It was fortunate that James came to Jurlique when he did. Once I decided that it was time to sell, I was keen to finalize the deal and remove myself from the big picture—thereby giving the new brooms plenty of room in which to sweep clean a passage for the new management. I had only two short meetings with Kerry and on each occasion gave him a quick rundown of the company's philosophy of "heart storming," and of how we were able to market effectively without spending a lot of money on it. I told him that, over two decades, we had developed a winning formula of pure, natural, organic, and spagyric health products, which was the perfect fit for a market that relied on cultural creatives and that wanted to break free of the plastic, synthetic, and unnatural world. Kerry said little, and left it to James to continue the discussion and to take care of the details prior to the acquisition. Once the takeover was signed by all partners, the Packer organization would then bring in their men to take over the books, and to set up new systems that would eventually break away from close networking into more mainstream marketing.

I have always believed that living is the journey, and not only the destination. However I had fallen into the trap of diminishing my happiness and satisfaction while running Jurlique on a daily basis. Unfortunately, most company CEOs perceive financial success as the measuring stick of value. But, of course, when you remove yourself from attachment and get outside the cage of the business model, you can see that there is much, much more to living than attaining benchmarks of money. For me, a big part of living was in the doing—and in "making a forest"—which involves planting and nurturing lots of strong trees. But just as producing products is important, a successful company needs to have leaders who can climb high, and contributors who will stay put when the going gets tough. As founder and leader of Jurlique for over twenty years, I saw that my contribution had peaked.

To go on doing the same things over and over and to somehow expect that there would be a different sort of result—well, that was not alchemic and not to the advantage of my further inner development. That was delusional thinking. Selling was the only option I had to get Jurlique to the next level. And fortunately, the exit terms that were later negotiated were neither dependent on my hands-on involvement nor, as I found out, on my consultancy.

In hindsight, I can see that I didn't have enough talent around me to take Jurlique up another rank as a global player. My wife was not involved strategically, and while she stayed involved with the company on a day-to-day basis during the first ten years, she was concerned with developing her personal dream and her skills as a fine art painter. Deep inside her heart, she was always a painter and a musician and was very gifted with both of these art forms. To bring up four children, to give them a good and safe start in life and to deal with the adversity of a hectic business took a lot of her time and energy. To her credit, she did do an outstanding job.

The employees of Jurlique in Australia and in the United States were passionate, reliable, and functioned well as the honest and efficient backbone for the company. But managers and executives never lasted long, with two or three exceptions. Darrel Lewis, my creative friend and the professional furniture manufacturer for Jurlique shops, used to ask me on a weekly basis—every time he entered the reception area—"Who is General Manager this week?" I had little time for the MBA type of manager who talks and e-mails well, and who enjoys his status and pay, but who—more often than not—disturbs the harmony of the day-to-day business by upsetting people in the short term and by inhibiting sales and profits in the long term. Think only about those young and inexperienced fund and investment managers in 2008 that helped to wreak havoc on the world financial system, small investors, and their pension funds in no time. Was that another "Generation Me" symptom?

I trusted the hard-working, consistent, efficient, and passionate workers and supervisors who were always permitted to speak up when managers created problems that the company did not normally have. The pool of managers and executives in Adelaide, South Australia, was not a very impressive list, so I preferred to give skilled and committed people the chance to work themselves up the ladder into managerial positions. Consequently, when the Packer organization got into the control seat, they were quick to install their own marketing and financial team. I only hoped that they would not damage the established niche brand by changing the fundamental design, packaging, vision, and principles of Jurlique for the sheer sake of change. Jurlique had a loyal band of supporters who would not be impressed by the stereotypical consultants who had "great new ideas" for a total change. Changes that haven't been thought through sufficiently reduce sales, profit, and the morale of both staff and customers—and can damage forever the established image of the company. Only a fool would want to change the logo, bottle, or image of Coca-Cola.

Before the Packer companies' offer became a done deal, I had some extraordinary encounters—and a very steep learning curve—caused by other so-called interested buyers. The first "serious" offer came around 1995 from a British-Australian group of investors based out of Sydney. At first they turned on a lot of charm, telling me how much they liked the quality of the Jurlique products and how they wanted to turn the company into the Rolls Royce of wellness. But when we got down to business, I was left flabbergasted at their offer—a dodgy credit line of three million dollars and the provision that they could cut and run within the first three years, but would take nearly total control of the company without any obligation to buy shares from Jurlique. What they proposed was a minefield of asset stripping and a fatal blow that would lead to the company's bankruptcy. In addition, they wanted to audit all the books before negotiations could even begin. At the time, Jurlique was making a small but respectable yearly profit. I looked in amazement as this investor group spoke about giving "a line of credit" for redeemable preference shares. Their way of doing business looked like the junk bond raiders on a smaller scale.

Another takeover offer came around the same time, from the same investors to a software company in Adelaide. I knew something was amiss when I couldn't contact that company offered as a reference. Finally, I determined that the company indicated as a reference had been raided by the same would-be investors. The takeover of that company had effectively destroyed it, forcing bankruptcy. I gratefully was warned and declined the deal.

There were some other bad experiences with potential investors. One was an Australian accountant "pimp" who somehow persuaded me to speak to his client, an Italian firm on the Adriatic Sea. I had to pay him an up-front consultant fee of fifteen thousand dollars, and he accompanied me to Italy where I was introduced to his Ferrari-driving master in a posh office, set up in a film studio. He acted like some sort of financial guru, raving about how he had financed railways in Russia and Vietnam and about his close friendship with the President of Kazakhstan and others. Perhaps he was a remote relative of Borat?

His offer was to buy out Jurlique for a few million dollars, and I politely asked how he intended to honor this cash commitment. His only reply was to mumble something about me signing a contract with him now, and that the cash would be held in some sort of account that I couldn't access without his agreement. He said that I had to hand over all of Jurlique's company shares. It didn't take me long to see that the flamboyant, grinning "investment-guru" was a con man.

Some other sell-out deals were genuine, but for various reasons didn't proceed. A quick deal with a famous Japanese cosmetic company to acquire Jurlique did not materialize because of their slowness to address the important issues of the sale. There was also a Swiss vitamin company involved with fish oil in Australia, which manufactured Omega 3 supplements. But when we got down to talking shares and cash, I found that they had fewer resources and were much smaller than Jurlique.

But perhaps the offer that I resented most, and for the longest time, came from a famous Sydney Investment Bank that wanted to own 51 percent of Jurlique for an insultingly low price. The impression I got from the bank negotiators and their top directors was that they had little respect for the hard work and success Jurlique had demonstrated, and even less respect for a scientist with a small beard who ran a flourishing company to its absolute peak. They were, nevertheless, impressed by facts and figures. We parted ways, miles apart in mind, perceptions, and values. Ten years later, the bank that once played big has lost most of its stock market value, just as Mr. Packer's companies have at the end of 2008.

After the Sydney Olympics, I was exhausted. The market selling price for Jurlique had gone from under $10 million to over $70 million. How much was Jurlique really worth? Another $10 million or perhaps more? The recurring thought kept going through my mind: "When is enough enough?" The buzz around Australia was that the Packer companies were about to clinch the "sale of the century" by jumping into the natural health industry. All the signs were there that they were planning to acquire Jurlique, and I accepted that it was the right time for me to finish what I had started.

A genuine, fine executive and gentleman in Sydney, by the name of Mark, contacted me and showed his respect and admiration for Jurlique. Mark was from one of the biggest and most respected accounting firms in the world, and he introduced me to James Packer and his executives. I was very impressed as he put all the cards on the table from the beginning, explaining how such a deal could be struck in a short time and in a fair and professional way. It was simply a question of negotiating Jurlique's net profit and the process required only a brief and proper diligence. What a breeze of fresh air it was to deal with a professional who held a passion and an admiration in his heart for all the hard, intelligent work we had done.

Perhaps what first sparked the Packers' interest in Jurlique was when I won two much publicized awards as the best entrepreneur of the year in the southern part of Australia. Was it that Kerry and James were impressed that a natural health scientist and businessman could win such awards? Or was it that they knew that the natural health and well-being industries were the fastest growing in the world? Or, that Jurlique was expanding quickly and had a marketing structure that didn't require a lot of investment, and that was already making bucket loads of cash? The fact that Jurlique was trading well in the black impressed James, as many of the Packer acquisitions required a cash bailout. For a casino devotee like Kerry Packer, Jurlique was a very safe bet.

Kerry and James Packer's first advice from their accountant was an evaluation that Jurlique's acquisition price was around $80 million. At the time, the PBL-owned Channel 9, a Packer company, was flying high after winning the live broadcasting rights for the Australian Football League. The AFL is the de facto religious organization for most of the Australian public. I knew that Kerry and James were proud of their recent success and I thought they were perhaps in a buying mood.

My first response was that the proposed buyout figure was a little low. Unperturbed, James sent a message that he would fly in his group of advisers on their own company jet to continue discussions. When I told the management and staff that James Packer would be coming to talk about the acquisition of Jurlique, everyone got into a bit of a tizzy, and I along with all our executives wore our best suits—and even ties—to greet our guests and possible new owners in style. To our surprise, James and his entire party turned up dressed in casual jeans, open shirts, and sneakers, as they wanted to embrace the simple lifestyle and relaxation of Jurlique. We all had a big laugh and fully enjoyed the pleasant meeting.

I introduced James to about 120 of the on-site and herb farm staffers. He was greeted with whistles and a buzz of excitement without anyone anticipating the dramatic staff changes that would take place later on. James was told that there were over 400 staff employed for the Australian operation, which included Jurlique concept spa stores, trainers, the head office in Mount Barker, the herbal processing factory, the QC laboratory, the administration, and the herb farm. The head office in the United States in Atlanta, Georgia employed over 150 executives and other staff. At the time, Jurlique was selling to twenty countries and nineteen exclusive distributors who sold tens of millions of pure health-care items every year. All of them together made Jurlique a $20 million net profit per year. When James heard the figures and the final sale price of Jurlique was negotiated, the evaluation went up to $146 million for 100 percent of Jurlique's shares. I finally settled for a total payout spread out over a five-year period. These figures where later published as news in the media, since the companies through which James and Kerry bought Jurlique where public companies with financial records available to the public.

While the financial terms were just acceptable, what pleased me most was to hear James say that the staff would not have to fear anything and that the company's vision and success would not be diminished in any way. The Packers' firm intention, according to James, was to expand the Jurlique range of products worldwide at an even faster rate. My staff took an immediate liking to the young, confident, and modest James who would soon inherit his father's fortune from an assortment of media, casino, and wellness industry interests. James rose to the occasion, loosened up, and praised the coming revolution of the health and well-being industry, of which Jurlique has proven to be a pioneer and a visionary.

Behind closed doors, James confided in me that he wanted to build Jurlique to achieve a one billion dollar turn over in business per year. "Can it be done, and in what time?" James asked.

"If you do it the right way, and follow my advice and the roots of Jurlique and don't get rid of the best people, it can be done in three to five years—provided enough capital is supplied for marketing, advertising, training, new distribution, education, and much more research and development," I replied.

With the deal done, all that was left was a meeting with Kerry, together with my daughter Thora, a director and manager of Jurlique Spa, training, and retail sales. We set off together to the CPH and PBL head office in Sydney. Kerry greeted us with a cigarette in one hand and a coffee cup grasped in the other. He said something about the health industry and addressed me as "young man," and I replied that I was only seven years younger than he was. He was astonished that through the health and well-being approach to life, despite the enormous stress in business, people could still stay and look young.

"So, James," he continued, "Tell me again, what is the profit, and how much cash do you have."

James responded, "Thirty-five percent net profit."

"That much! It can't be done by a scientist," Kerry loudly retorted.

Thora instantly replied humorously and quickly, as was her usual way, "My father is known as a white Jew."

Kerry roared with loud laughter. "The white Jew."

The expression came from our closest German and Jewish friend, Charlotte Schwenzner. Charlotte was a wise and spiritual Grand Dame in Adelaide, aged over ninety but sharp and humorous as a young girl. She nearly died in Hitler's Nazi Germany, but escaped to Australia and was morally and financially a big helper to Jurlique when the Klein Family arrived in Adelaide in 1984.

"You understand tax, then," said Kerry. "How much tax do you pay?"

James advised, "The usual."

"How much?" Kerry wanted to know.

"Seven million," said James.

"Well then," paused Kerry. "We'll have to talk to Y and E."

The last time I saw Kerry was at a party with his executives. It was in a huge tent erected close to his house on the Sydney North Shore. Kerry was sitting on a sofa and James introduced me to his sister, who was sitting next to her father. She was interested and involved in natural health, and we had a short discussion. Rock music was playing outside and Kerry didn't look very well. He asked if there was anything he could do about his grave health problems. "Yes, I said carefully, there is always a treatment with alternative and complementary medicine." But I knew that Kerry trusted only his conventional doctors for medical advice.

My last words to Kerry Packer were that nature provides for everything. "For everything you do to yourself, there is a natural way that can override the negative effects of an unhealthy lifestyle, sickness and the aging process."

When I left Jurlique in 2003, the company's accumulated revenue in the previous year—from all the Jurlique businesses of exported products, Australian wholesale, U.S. sales, and the Jurlique concept spas and wellness stores—was about $100 million, up from $86,000 in 1985. The Jurlique bank account had a prudent accumulative reserve of $7 million—all the cash flow it could ever need—and a net profit of $20 million per year. That was Solomon's gift I left behind, along with the knowledge that Jurlique, the child, had blossomed holistically into a healthy corporate adult. I wished the new owners all success, benefits, and goodwill from my brain and heart child of twenty years.

CHAPTER 13

Letting Go of the Whole

When I was in the laboratory working spagyrically with plants, minerals, and metals, I knew how to separate, clarify, and combine substances so that the whole could become more than the sum of its original parts. A similar situation occurs when a natural physician looks into the holistic state of a patient and finds a mental or psychological disorder. This disorder, or mental sickness, won't show up in a diagnosis device, used to measure the patient's antibody levels, or in any other machinery. This is because the wellness of a human being is interconnected with his or her nature, which is organic, psychic, mental and not only mechanical. Health and nature are synonymous as they originate from the same organic source and life force. The reason why, with few exceptions, a person gets into a state of disease is that, holistically, the human being has become separated from her or his whole. This lack of wholeness is the cause of disunity, which manifests as a disease, from a common cold to a cancerous growth.

A parallel situation of disorder arises in business when a company changes owners and management. The former owner—if he hangs on until the bitter end—does so oblivious to the fate of the company and its future. One of the major problems of modern business is that the top management executives are obsessed with analysis and pay very little attention to the incorporated holistic design model. And, unfortunately, what is little understood by executives and company leaders is that the manufacturing of products, and the ensuing trading that follows, is contingent on the demand of the public. Their perception of the products is directly related to the human design, which is governed by thoughts that are associated with the heart's deep inner feelings.

Staying on temporarily as the CEO of Jurlique after effectively handing over the control and the checkbook to the new management and owners, I was left with a feeling of emptiness and disappointment that needed to be filled with a new cycle of activity and creativity. This sense of meaninglessness was exacerbated by the disintegration of my marriage of thirty-two years, which resulted in the sad alienation of my wife and four adult children, all of whom had been raised in their new country of Australia from childhood. As a family we had lived and thrived together, and now we were moving apart at a time when ideally we could have been collectively celebrating our hard-earned success. I had acquired more wealth than I could possibly have expected or even dreamed of when we first arrived in Australia twenty years earlier. What was disturbing to me was that while on the one hand I was locked up with feelings of disappointment and emptiness, on the other hand the media was honoring me for being a brilliant achiever, and listing me in Australia's top 150 rich and famous people.

In a close relationship, one can only be happy and forgiving when both partners accept themselves and the other as they are. For me that was always the case, and I was mostly content with what I got from the relationship. However, Ulrike seemed to be in a continuous struggle with what I was and what I represented. The separation process from Ulrike was extremely draining. I did not handle this debilitating situation well, and I did not want it to drag on any longer than was absolutely necessary. Fortunately, we both kept the terms of our separation from being a highly publicized battle. As with many women of our time who have decided to separate from a relationship that for them is no longer acceptable, Ulrike had made up her mind. It seems to me that in relationships, men are resolute to the point of disbelief when the couple falls apart. I agreed to everything without any battle. In my mind, I was the creator of all Jurlique's ideas, inventions, and innovations. I had carried the business burden on a daily basis all the time, and had not always been supported by my now ex-wife, especially during the final stages when leaving the company.

At certain times, the intensity of brokering the deal to sell

Jurlique at the same time as the brisk, unexpected separation from my wife brought me (and the company) to the brink of collapse. But I had a secret solution that was used most effectively to raise the total selling price from $80 million to $146 million. This secret was Dr. Edward de Bono's "Six Thinking Hats Method," which is a tool of lateral and parallel thinking.

Like everyone else who gets the opportunity to experience the value of the Six Thinking Hats, I was intrigued as to how it had used such simple knowledge to brilliantly impact human consciousness and negotiations. During the launch of the new de Bono and J. Lyons book, *Marketing Without Money*, in which I was prominently featured, de Bono met my daughter, Thora, and me for lunch in Adelaide. During our long conversation, Dr. de Bono explained to us how in all business transactions, complex argumentative thinking and talking were the biggest stumbling blocks. He went on to further explain that the basic idea behind all Western thinking was designed about two thousand three hundred years ago by what he referred to as the "Greek gang of three." Their design, based on argument and dialectic, has caused the misery of our time in the form of capitalism, communism, and violence that has destroyed millions of people and put the planet in peril.

The first wave of the argumentative and confrontational approach to problem solving came when Socrates placed great emphasis on dialectic and argument. In 80 percent of the dialogues in which he was involved, there was no constructive outcome at all. Socrates saw his role as simply pointing out what was "wrong." Plato and Aristotle continued the legacy of confrontation by advocating that the "ultimate" truth be hidden below appearances. His famous analogy is of a person chained up in a cave with a fire at the entrance that creates shadows on the back wall of the cave. The person can only see the shadows, and not the reality. Plato cleverly used this analogy to point out, somewhat absurdly, that we all go through life seeing only the "shadows" of the truth. This idea of shadows in the mind led to heated debate about who's right and who's wrong. Finally, Aristotle added to the genre of combative thinking by systemizing the logic of inclusion and exclusion. In his system, all past experiences and memories of the brain were stored in boxes so that everything could be judged by its box.

This tragic Greek legacy of thought has continued mostly unchallenged into the twenty-first century, with the consequence that today most people are only concerned with "what is"—being the material determined by previously recorded analysis, prejudice, and argument. The solution for the combative thinking problem—the root cause of all war and disagreements—can only be solved by thinking about "what can be" rather than "what is." The shift in thinking, according to Edward de Bono, is to design our way into the future instead of judging our way there.

If you read the daily newspapers or watch the news on TV, you will see that everything is presented reactively. Reporters are taught to only write stories that will trigger people's reactive thinking. Ratings are basically the tally board of viewer's reactions. The media gets its desired reaction by focusing on human conflicts and the emotional dramas played out in the world's major disagreements.

But in parallel thinking, which is the opposite of vertical, linear thinking, all views—no matter how contradictory—are made parallel. If, later on, it is essential to choose between the different positions, then a choice is made at that point. If a choice cannot be made, then the design has to cover both possibilities. The whole value of parallel thinking is that the experience and intelligence of everyone can be used in each direction. Parallel thinking makes the fullest use of everyone's intelligence and experience; nobody's opinion is suppressed, ridiculed, or discarded.

Many people say that they enjoy arguments because they can show off how clever they are, and that would be acceptable if humanity was still stuck surviving under the laws of jungle warfare. But, we have evolved as species—we have flown to the moon and we live in civilizations. What is this need to continue thinking like primitive hunters, demolishing opponents with argument and debate? In parallel thinking, a person shows off by showing how many considerations he or she can put forward under the various categories of "colored hats."

De Bono showed me that ever since Freud, the emphasis has been on analysis to find the deep truths and motivations for action. The approach of Chinese Confucianism was the polar opposite. Instead of focusing on personality, Confucius chose to focus directly on the behavioral influence exuded by people on their colleagues, subordinates, superiors, and family members. Confucius wasn't one bit interested in a person's psychological makeup. He wasn't concerned with what the thinker thought, or in solving his madness of thinking through memory analysis. He was only concerned with what the thinker did with his or her thoughts.

The Thinking Hats Method, as taught by Dr. de Bono, follows the Confucian approach rather than the Western analytical approach. The rules of behavior in a group problem-solving discussion are laid out clearly, and each person acts out his or her own emotional states and thought-feelings in accordance with only the color used at that time. Each color represents a defined way of how to contribute to a discussion without arguing. (Color therapy also plays a prominent role in my new innovation, the JK7-Spa Sensator, which is discussed later).

Edward de Bono used the analogy of a magnet that is only powerful because all of its particles are aligned in the same direction. Such alignment does not occur in an argument or a free discussion. In an argument, a person holds back important information because of the fear that he or she might lose the argument and lose face. (China and other parts of Asia have a strong cultural belief in the axiom "Never lose face," which Mao exploited cruelly against his people). This is a reflection of how aberrant—and damaging—the human ego can be to the goals of collaboration and problem solving. At first, the whole concept of the Six Thinking Hats sounded terribly simplistic and even childishly immature. But once I completed a short course on the technique, I was genuinely amazed by the effectiveness of the concept and by how brilliantly simple it was to understand and use.

As Dr. de Bono explained it to me there were two main purposes to the Six Thinking Hats concept. The first was to simplify thinking by allowing a thinker to deal with one thing at a time. The second was to switch to separate modes of thinking. The technique effectively takes care of emotions, logic, information, and creativity one after the other. Like in alchemy, a competent practitioner of the Six Thinking Hats can relate to the separation of thinking and emotional components before bringing them back together, and can then orchestrate a quick agreement between the discussion participants or between the buyer and the seller. By being able to switch to different modes of thinking, the heat of the negotiation isn't intense or threatening. In a negotiation without the customary rigid formalities, preconceived notions, and unreasonable conditions cannot dominate.

Dr. de Bono rattled off many examples of numerous companies that had used his method of the Six Thinking Hats to find rapid solutions to serious problems. One example was when Statoil in Norway had a serious problem and no apparent solution: an oilrig was costing one hundred thousand dollars a day. After the Six Hats method was used, in a period of only twelve minutes, the problem was solved and the costs were reduced to nil. In another situation, IBM found that the Six Thinking Hats reduced meeting times to one quarter of what they used to be. In an experiment with three hundred senior civil servants, the introduction of the Six Hats increased thinking productivity by almost 500 percent. Schoolteachers reported getting amazing results by teaching the method to four- and five-year-olds, while the big corporate players like Microsoft, NASA, IBM, Du Pont, Shell and BIP, as well as Federal Express, all used the Six Hats for problem solving with remarkable success.

    I questioned Dr. de Bono about why the Six Thinking Hats worked so effectively—almost magically. He explained how in normal arguments, more politely called debates, if someone says something, then others have to respond—even if only out of politeness or friendship. But with the parallel thinking method of the Six Hats—used at one meeting during one conversation—all participants are thinking at each moment and the momentum is in the same direction. The thoughts are laid out in parallel with no response or rebuttal given to the previous person's thought, thereby neither validating nor invalidating the power or influence of former arguments. Instead of residual entrapment, one simply adds another idea in parallel. In the end, the subject is fully explored from six angles of thought and feeling, and quick decision making occurs by orchestrating consent for a solution.

    In normal business negotiations, if two points of view are in conflict they are argued out. Some lose, some win, and the arguments are often decided by bossing and bullying. People like to show off their egos and oftentimes, confrontational and adversarial thinking are used to attack and put down one another. But with parallel thinking, both points of view are laid out alongside each other. Without argument, decisions can be reached amicably with every step forward. Under the thinking umbrella of the Six Colored Hats, any matter of contention can be explored and solved in a very short time. This is something arguments and reasoning cannot do.

Like all games in life, regardless of the perceived importance—whether it be for survival or entertainment—the Six Thinking Hats have some basic rules to master. However, the methodology is that there are six colors, each of which creates an image of a solution that, in turn, leads to a constructive outcome. Each color relates to a function of how people think and feel, as explained by de Bono:

* White Hat is neutral and objective and concerned with objective facts and figures.
* Red Hat suggests anger, rage, and the honest expression of emotions.
* Black Hat is seriously cautious, critical, and careful.
* Yellow Hat is sunny, positive, and hopeful.
* Green Hat is creative abundance and fertile growth.
* Blue Hat is cool and in control, creating the foundation for the thinking process. It orchestrates the manner in which the other hats are used.

In my protracted negotiations for the sale of Jurlique, each time we reached a potential stumbling point I would quietly think through the Six Thinking Hats myself, and then select a functional color to ride through the negative inputs and emotional hindrances to find solutions. At one point, when some of James Packer's accountants appeared to equivocate over the final payment that involved millions of dollars, I reached inside myself for the de Bono red hat, and told them how angry and humiliated I felt. I then stormed out of the office in a controlled rage and said that I would come back in ten minutes. When I returned smiling twenty minutes later, I showed myself wearing the sunny yellow hat, expressing, that I had nothing to lose. The positive outflow defused a situation that threatened to not only spoil the party but also to shut down the entire sale. By the skillful use of parallel thinking, I got over the last hurdle and both parties perceived the final selling price of Jurlique as acceptable and fair. "Cool Blue" finally led us to what we all wanted.

Dr. de Bono wasn't just a thinking genius. He passed on the wisdom that, in business, it's dangerous to outwardly expose personal mountains or achievements. The smart play is to hold the mountains of success within, so that people don't get jealous or resentful. De Bono was tremendously intelligent in his understanding of the mental design of concepts. His articulation of the brain as the hardware for the mind is still as revolutionary as Krishnamurti was before him, and I am sure that history will judge him alongside Newton and Einstein for changing the way people perceive how the world works. What Dr. de Bono articulates so well is the safe way for people to change and thrive together.

But even with parallel thinking, the Six Thinking Hats,

and the wisdom I had gained from great masters as well as from my own extensive practical experiences, none of this left me with any sense of deeper freedom as I prepared to leave my Jurlique family. Despite the millions of dollars from the sale, the idea that money, power, and the lack of time for me and for others could replace a lifetime of work and commitment from the heart caused me annoyance and uneasiness. All pragmatism fades away when confronted by pure mental clarity and objective heart-driven feelings and emotions. This sense of finality, compounded with the unwanted split from my family, sent me into long periods of introspective thought, struggle, sorrow, and self-pity—I was suffering from a severe case of the "poor me" syndrome.

"Where is the reason and the value?" I asked. "When does money have value, and when does the value of money work in harmony with inner values?" These questions filled my mind, and the agitation became so intense that all I could see was a big signpost saying STOP to all of the past. The deal was done, and I just had to get away and find some new space.

Throughout all my adult life, I had never known any major sickness. This was due mostly to the natural health regime I religiously kept through swimming, yoga, and meditation, as well as eating natural, organic healthy foods and no meat for a long time. The circumstances before and after the sale of Jurlique had shaken my body's physical foundation; my body now housed all my sad feelings and mental patterns that I relied on for my life and direction. I knew that either needed to take decisive action to transform my life and start a new cycle or I would suffer from a psychosomatically derived disease soon. I was on the brink of a debilitating and long midlife crisis.

Apart from taxes and death, the one other certainty I knew about life was the law of karma and retribution, which, even for a critical, nature-loving scientist, is the understanding that for every cause, there is an equal effect. I might be able to believe that I was done with Jurlique—but I asked myself, "Is Jurlique karmically done with me?" The solution was to transform or even transmute, and get on with the beginning of a new life.

But as I departed from my adopted country, Australia, the anxiety and frustrations of ending a long partnership with my now ex-wife began to overflow. The final chapter reached closure as I let go of what was a huge portion of our lives together as a family. As painfully as letting go can be, I now realize that nothing lasts forever in this short span that we call one life, and we all will take *nothing* with us when we die, which could be anytime.

I called my travel agent and booked a flight to central Asia with Darrel and Weibei, who had graciously and passionately contributed to the health and wealth of Jurlique for many years. The journey took us on the remote Silk Road through China, and to the ancient alchemy sites of Bukara, Kiva, Samarkant, and Tashkent in Uzbekistan. I spent several weeks revisiting and reestablishing my roots, and immersing myself in the knowledge of alchemy and transformation. All of this led some of my energy back to balance and harmony, and enabled me to let the past go and focus on the Now.

Finally, for a new direction, I felt my heart's compass directing me to the top of one of the six holy mountains of China: Hua Shan. I could feel the excitement of a new future on the horizon. We flew to Moscow, Petersburg, and finally to Berlin, my country of origin. All thoughts of the selling of Jurlique had been left behind, and somehow were transformed into a new energy pattern of renewal. For the first time in more than thirty years, I felt a sudden rush of relaxed happiness—even exhilaration—mixed with an inner wisdom that something remarkable was going to happen. Little did I know that waiting for me in Berlin was a soul mate that was destined to become the greatest love of my life, and my new wife.

CHAPTER 14

CRISIS OF FAITH

Is there a tipping point, a catalyst, or perhaps some unknown phenomenon that causes a crisis of faith during a human lifetime? Or is it that in a far greater reality, one life is part of a short journey? Perhaps when one's journey finally reaches a perceived destination or termination point, beings that possess sufficient consciousness become like mental supernovae, beautifully destroying the past, which had filled everything with negativity. Stars burst, signaling the start of another journey of discovery. If this is true, and a person is reborn again and again in his or her nontemporary form, then it's possible that during one lifetime, a person can evolve and holistically transform for a greater purpose that cannot be logically understood by a human mind that thinks only linearly.

When one cycle in life ends, it's difficult to focus on the transformation that's taking place. For those people who push their own limits and are prepared to jump out of the box of restricted and conditioned thinking, the process of letting go can be both a riveting and liberating experience. However, it can be terrifying at the same time to realize that to transform it's necessary to virtually kill your old ego/self. Without an understanding of how the transformation process happens, a person can easily spiral into a crisis of faith, questioning and doubting everything he has known and accepted as truth. To let go of a life's work and family is like a snail leaving behind its shell and facing the world in a naked and seemingly vulnerable state. In this situation, only two choices are possible: either to change or to fade away into meaninglessness.

At first, I felt the frustration of trying to find some anchorage and grounding. It is not enough to know that "it's over when it's over"—the finality doesn't become a reality or a truth until a person first experiences the emptiness it leaves in the heart. This emptiness has extreme effects on the body, mind, and spirit. I firmly believe that I would have been unable to take the high road and ride my life to a new level if I had not been equipped with some tried-and-true tools to overcome this negative edge.

My protection against negativity was the valuable arsenal of my daily mental and physical health regime. In times of crisis, healthy habits instilled by decades of practice can prevent a holistic disintegration—not an uncommon occurrence as evidenced by the large number of male CEOs who die prematurely in the first two years after their mandatory retirements or being fired. These prematurely deceased beings had been keeping themselves alive with the purpose and convictions of their life's occupation. Therefore they believed that their retirement meant that their "used by" date had been exceeded, triggering negative thoughts and feelings and ultimately the death process. Rather than ending one cycle and starting afresh, most retirees who exit their life's work in their sixties stop there. They do not see that they should still should have decades of active living ahead of them.

For these high achievers, the letting go process can be a fatal blow. They are sent into the isolated abyss where they surrender to darkness—resulting in sorrow, disease, and early death. The psychic condition of stress, depression, and fear will certainly lead down a fast road, plastered with impotence and chronic diseases like serious heart problems, Alzheimer's, Parkinson's, Prostate Cancer. Stress and its psychosomatic consequences are slowly seen and diagnosed by the more rigid traditionalists in medicine. Only deep relaxation and meditation can serve as tools for change. This is not seen as quack business anymore! This is the exact area where I felt I would be able to help and contribute with a new invention.

When a person makes the decision to live holistically, over time, self-doubts may be transformed into a quality of faith and wisdom. This can enable a person to face his or her fears of worthiness, and restore a sense of confidence to complete all of life's cycles. But the primary fear everyone must face during the cycles of being, which complete a full and meaningful life, is the fear of letting go. Once the letting go process is allowed to blossom then all thoughts of a singular termination point quickly vanish from one's mind.

Once a person can look beyond the past, they become fortified with the understanding that the past is no longer real. The past is gone forever, but energy and thoughts do exist in the Now so we aren't stuck in distorted past-time conditioning. Present time energy can be created and determined instantly in real time without carrying the baggage of history. What's always true is that solutions come when the time is right, and that the puzzles of life become much less serious, more intuitive, and less reactive when a person is able to reach out and connect to what the Chinese refer to as the Tao, the primordial energy source. This is the life force that opens the window of insight that spins life's cycles into natural fruition, free of fear and sorrow. It just is as it is, and the future and past have no relevance in the present time.

As my journey with Jurlique approached the departure point I took time out for some introspection, and delved into the latest writing of Deng Ming-Dao. Ming-Dao wrote the landmark novel, *The Secret Life of A Taoist Master*, as well as *365 Tao: Daily Meditations*. In the deep reflective state that his writing inspired, I was able to distinguish the now-essence from past illusions and naïve hope for a better future. I was able to reconnect to the powerful Eastern teachings of "qi," which emphasize the importance of physical and energetic movement. My experience was enriched by the physical rhythm of swimming long distances every day, some mental strength exercises designed for enhancing well-being and longevity, and reading time and again the same insightful and wise texts from Krishnamurti, Eckhart Tolle, Deng Ming-

Dao, and the I-Ching.

When a person is immersed in the emptiness of termination, food is also an important weapon to keep the mind free from the implosions of negativity energy. I am convinced that human beings become what they eat and think, and that what goes into the body system is alchemically transformed both physically and energetically into various material and metaphysical states. For as long as I can remember I have always believed—through experience—that the best staple diet for human beings is vegetable and fruits mixed with herbs and fish protein, as well as the essential prodigestive oils of whole nut kernels.

Whenever possible, I have refrained from eating animals, and not only as an act of compassion for animal rights, which is an undeniably worthy cause. Rather, because of my knowledge acquired through thirty years of research, I have found the best ways to keep down my body's toxicity levels. Just as nicotine smoke clogs blood vessels and damages the lungs and the whole body, the flesh and blood from suffering animals damages the purity of the human digestive system. Unnecessary strain is put on the pancreas, liver, kidneys, and heart, and other organs are forced to work overtime when toxicity implodes on our vulnerable body. It's no coincidence that meat eaters have more heart attacks and colon cancer than vegetarians do, or that they suffer more from anger and emotional disorders. Because of the pain and brutal slaughter of animals, a karmic payback does appear to transpose onto meat-eating human beings the form of sickness and negative emotional thinking.

Most diseases can be related directly to diet, and there is much truth to the adage, "we are what we eat" (as well as, "death sits in and acts from the intestine"). Humans could reach a biologically normal age of between 100 and 120 years and could be fit and healthy, if we faced neither mental pressures that cause fear nor the addiction to drugs, junk food, and sweet soda drinks that dramatically shorten lives. Global food giants and the powerful pharmaceutical and medical lobbies—in conjunction with weak or corrupt government agencies—are doing a good job to get rid of ever-more-quickly aging people.

My foundational belief system was formed on an understanding and passion for holistic health modalities and the alchemic transformation of organic and inorganic substances. I had spent half of my life designing and selling spagyrically based products that made people look great and feel better. This was the material extension of a highly attuned belief system that was empowered by the goodness of nature. Such belief was in a totally different quadrant to most business executives who build their beliefs on greed and ruthlessness, with the singular purpose of dominating and profiting in the marketplace. The modern workplace is an extension of the Roman gladiatorial arena, complete with lots of superficial games, sorrow, and blood.

During my tenure at the helm of Jurlique, I steered a radical passage that avoided useless and destructive confrontation and competition. The Jurlique label achieved a worldwide reputation for zero tolerance of impurity in its products distributed for public consumption. The bottom line for Jurlique's success was a strategy of collaboration and cooperation with the wellness culture. Since the 1980s, Jurlique has been a part of influencing people to think holistically, and not mechanically, through preventive medicine. This allows for the restoration and maintenance of optimum wellness and healthy living habits.

As I began to let go of Jurlique, which occupied so much of my life and passions, the past began to fragment and dissolve into lines of new imagery. I began to see an emergence of new patterns. Intuitively, I reasoned that at some future time—after the letting go process—there would be a new opportunity for reconnection and renewal of my long relationship with the natural health industry. A whole new range of treatments and spagyric health products flashed through my mind. I could sense that the old self had already began to expire, and my enquiring mind asked, "What's next?"

After the decision to leave Jurlique was finalized, I preferred to believe that the letting go process, to the astonishment of family and friends, must be completed in the shortest possible timeline. But the reality is that all the karma of the past isn't subject to the mind's fixed idea of psychological time scales. Sometimes, as I was about to discover, the karmic laws and residues of life's energy can result in a crisis of faith that can rip through the heart, and pierce the essential spirit that keeps the human species one step ahead of the animal realm. While letting go can bring about a reality check in "now time," for me, the process brought to a head all the perceived weakness, insincerity, and hypocrisy of my past business, family life, and the existing wellness culture.

As much as I wanted to remain positive toward a cultural movement that embraced natural living and organic nonchemical products, the letting go of Jurlique and much of my life's work seemed to become water under the bridge. I faced what seemed to be a highly competitive and uninspiring wellness industry. Would wellness ever be able to make the transformation from being culturally dependent into a generally accepted belief that natural health is good for everyone—the young and the old, the healthy and the sick? I questioned the role that wellness could realistically play in solving earth's immediate problems.

Such reoccurring thoughts flooded my mind—so much so that I thought, without a radical generational change, wellness would become a pop group without an audience, existing as a wind-up clock in the digital age. I desperately wanted to defend my chosen path and life's work from my own crisis of faith, but mentally, I was adrift in a storm that was lashing the foundations of my being. This negativity, along with my painful experiences with my ex-wife and the new Jurlique owners, dug deep down into my heart like a dagger in pursuit. How long did I have to suffer this time?

In hindsight they all just did what they were able to understand and do, which now seems quite okay. Even at the time, I was grateful for the fast separation process that was taking place and changing my life for the better. I began to catch a future vision of how the wellness culture that had taken root globally would become a life-enhancing experience for others and me. Public perception changed from the old confrontational energies, based on a conventional medical and pharmaceutical lobby. These old ideas slowly faded to clear the pathway for a way of life based on preventative natural medicine and the maintenance of good health and real healing.

From the depths of a debilitating upheaval provoked by the difficulty of letting go, a new clarity emerged. Suddenly, I could envision people from all belief systems coming together to learn and practice holistic wellness in a manner suited to their needs and preferences, their evolution, and their interdependent path on earth. I began to see a new era of wellness and a better, cleaner living environment, an epoch which would arrive in real time on earth like a pebble landing onto a still pond, creating ripples of health for people and the planet that would go on until reaching the far edge of time, which is always only in the now.

Understanding wellness as holistic ripples brought clarity and pushed me toward the critical point at which I would either let go and flow into a new life, or remain embroiled with the old energy, dependent on recalled memories. My mind probed more and more deeply into what makes life satisfying, and I realized that unconditional love was the only real love. How was it that wellness continued to blossom while the quality of most popular foods and drinks for public consumption had deteriorated? Why was there no such thing as a healthy coke? Why were most of the supermarkets, which fed billions of people every day, filling their shelves with processed, unhealthy "dead" and "super-sizing" foods? And was it that the natural health industry, with all its hype and public relations, had been unable to change the perception of food from being seen as an addictive, taste-orientated body fuel? Unhealthy food is turning half of the world's population into "sicko fatties," while the other half is starving to death in poverty, or living dangerously with polluted water, soil, and air.

Clearly something was amiss, and the fact that I was seeing all this so clearly at a time when I was terminating my role as a wellness leader seemed far more than just a coincidence. I felt hurt, resentful, and hopeless, as I had spent so many years of my life as a leader and advocate of the natural health and wellness culture. I also felt a sense of responsibility mixed with shame for being part of an industry that had masked its shortfalls to conform to standards of the profit-oriented business world. A large health food chain in America, with a history of idealism and passion, had been so helpful in the early Jurlique days. It has since been gobbled up, along with dozens of other businesses, by a few greedy and hypocritical "big biz" players. Has not the same happened to the wellness industry, wherein day and resort spas cater to the rich, with expensive design and mediocre service? What was once a genuine motivation to offer caring treatments to stressed and sick people seems to have become just another new way to get loads of fast cash and desired centers of profit.

Fortunately, my mind's "critical black hat" observation of how things are, and what the risk is for change, turned into my yellow and green thinking hats. This provided me with some clear perception of where to go. I then realized the enormous potential of "nutraceuticals," the chemical and drug-free pharmaceuticals that were the new buzz, being a realistic alternative to medical cocktails and the artificial sugar-laden junk drinks. As a scientist and alternative medical health practitioner, I had wisely founded the charitable Klein Foundation with the complimentary Klein Research Institute (KRIL) during the heydays of Jurlique. This enabled me to legally put away millions of pretax profits into an organization that carried out genuine research. It proved scientifically that herbal medicines and nutraceuticals work brilliantly as antioxidants, and have other functions against the free radical scavengers that are known for causing cancer and other diseases.

I felt that now was the time to use this tool wisely to create a new level of health products. The coming era of new wellness would be the critical time for all people to save themselves and the planet from human-made pollutants and excesses. Solving problems from within would create a ripple effect that would benefit a suffering planet and its ailing population in need of a natural fix.

In my mind's eye, the strength of the new wellness ripples would lead to all the big and powerful multinational soda companies to transform their dangerous sugar-filled soft drinks into tasty health tonics, laced with Echinacea and sweet natural stevia along with other healing herbs. Furthermore, all natural, organic, and herbal ingredients would replace artificial chemicals in all foods. Most importantly, hydrogen fuel cells and hydrogen from seawater would replace carbon combustion energy, and put a fast and final end to the oil era of rampant pollution, global warming, insane profits, and oil-driven wars.

Projecting such a future into the present, I could see a whole range of new products and services including the extraction of the natural chemical goodness of green tea and even coffee, thereby amplifying the original benefit tenfold. Vegetables would be naturally and spagyrically treated and cooked to taste like animal steaks, to wean humanity away from the toxic, addictive, and cruel meat business. The next wellness wave would not only revolutionize people's perceptions about health and longevity but, in time, would completely transform the way humanity coexists on a small, fragile planet in the outer suburbs of a spiraling galaxy.

All this insight sounds logical and realistic in the sense that, as a species, humanity is totally dependent on earth's sustainability for survival. Without a harmonious relationship with earth, the human species faces the prospect of becoming extinct. The planet will survive regardless of what we do, and will recover easily—with caring humans or without. In a few hundred years, everything will balance again in harmony and beauty. The planet doesn't need us humans to survive, but as a dependent species we need our planet to survive. We need to care for and make peace with our earth.

My vision into the near decades ahead included health food shops lining all streets and displaying a distinctive holistic-certified branding. "Why is it," I asked, "that despite all the cosmetic success of health foods today, there is no unequivocal validation that health foods do actually save people's lives?" This lack of positive proof stems from the United States' Federal Drug and Food Association (FDA), a powerful group heavily influenced by the global food, pharmaceutical, and medical lobby. The FDA asserts the unfounded assumptions that no natural products on earth could possibly treat life-threatening diseases such as diabetes and cancer. But the FDA grudgingly accepts that some strong antioxidants can complement—and even assist with—the treatment of serious diseases.

The conservative, outdated views of the FDA as well as those of the World Health Organization (WHO) have resulted in the health industry being cornered into a no-win (no-health) situation. All legitimate, certified health interests are being muffled and forced to capitulate to medical standards that are biased toward drugs and hospitals. Indeed, there is a huge sickness industry that isn't interested in the pursuit of health and wellness. The regulations don't, however, stop clever business people from pushing so-called health products with claims like, "Guaranteed to extend your life and sexual prowess by twenty years." Smart companies with huge financial reserves are exploiting loopholes to keep their products "alive" for long periods—before they are inevitably forced to change their outrageous labeling and often-deadly side effects.

Today the health industry is subjected to the falsity of quality controls, as is evidenced by fruit extracts used to manufacture "natural" vitamins. Naturally, every plant and tree sucks up all essential ingredients from the ground. But when the soil is depleted of all nutrients, what they suck up is mostly water and chemical fertilizers without any of the earth's original goodness. They may be grown organically, but most vegetables sold today in the supermarkets and leading health food stores—like tomatoes and carrots—have only a fraction of the nutrients they had fifty years ago. Why is there no information or labeling showing that the food being sold today is nearly empty of all nutrients? Such heavily "enriched" food, stuffed full of chemical additives, is ideal to fill up on to become fat and sick. The truth is that dead food is the primary cause of obesity and diabetes. But the FDA isn't concerned, and most general practitioners couldn't care less. They would much rather prescribe and profit from billions of dollars of drug prescriptions that treat some symptoms, and invariably create more problems and post-treatment sickness.

The truth—which isn't seen on any labeling—is that 60 to 70 percent of all cancer comes from pollution and deplorably inadequate nutrition. Over the last one hundred years, humanity has maintained a constant pillaging of all the essential nutrients from the earth's soil, water, and air. The health of humans is reliant upon new breakthroughs in natural medicines such as Xanthones and polyphenols, the super powerful antioxidants found in tropical fruits and sea creatures. These may yet become one of the best proactive treatments for cancer and other diseases.

My crisis of faith, which eventually turned from severe doubt to a renewed belief that health is the true wealth, initially came about when the Packer family took over the reins of Jurlique. This released me from the driver's seat of Australia's most respected natural cosmetic and health brand. The change in role transformed my public status from being the chief executive of one of Australia's most dynamic independent companies into an exciting "New CEO" with a light golden parachute and a new life to live.

Under a five-year buyout deal, the Packer group would take up less than 50 percent of the shareholding, leaving the remaining half to two investors in the United States that would each take out allotments of 25 percent. James Packer informed me that he had two billionaire friends with ownership in, and prime connection to, the exploding nature-based health industry. They were interested in buying into and "loving" Jurlique. It was obvious to everyone that the baby Jurlique had now grown up, and was taking a new direction into the fast lane of a healthy global expansion.

It was time for a new cycle and that also meant an end to my thirty-two-year marriage to Ulrike. She decided to keep a minority shareholding stake in the company we both started. To prevent any acrimony, we divided all the gains and assets equally, and I prepared to leave my company, home, wife, and four independent and grown children. Nevertheless, our separation came as a shock to my children and was unexpected to me. But now my only wish is to keep the positive memories and be grateful for such a harsh yet rewarding change.

In the Chinese calendar I was classified as the fast moving monkey—purportedly the smartest animal on earth. But despite the monkey in me, I had learned to curtail my propensity for egotism and instead learned to mindfully avoid the limelight and the media. I never set up interviews for TV programs; the presenters and producers came to us. I kept away from showmanship in my business dealings. However, as the final days with Jurlique ran their course, the media was always chasing me for the big story of my relationship with the Packer family and my breakup with Ulrike. While I declined all interviews, that didn't stop one magazine report from referring to me as the Bill Gates of the wellness industry. My press persona went from being the "Golden Apple" of natural health to the Richard Branson of a new world-class wellness industry. While the media circled in a frenzy, I had only one thought cycling through my mind: How could I exit Jurlique in the best way possible, and then let it go forever?

Jurlique's products were beautiful from the inside out, with unique design and packaging that expressed itself through its colors. Real gold symbolized preciousness and high value, blue symbolized high wisdom, and white symbolized elegance, class and cleanliness. For me, Jurlique was worth much more than cash in the bank. One alchemist friend said that I had fulfilled an alchemist's dream in the twenty-first century by making gold (capital) from water and lotions, and not from lead, as was purportedly the traditional way of manufacturing gold centuries ago.

I was nearly sixty years of age, but my body and mind still functioned like a forty-year-old—even with the enormous stress and workload I had endured for twenty-five years. While walking the talk and living the holistic lifestyle, I had trouble handling all the stress from the people around me. My problems were less related to my own health than to the health of those who surrounded me. I had allowed the company to hang onto its old structure, which did not mesh with the slick Packer Corporation. The Packers thrived on people being competitive, and company decisions were made through the drilled ranks of management and executive's control. I was much more lateral and creative in my thinking than those executives who surrounded me. Rather than trying to educate them, I decided to leave the newcomers alone—at their request—to discover for themselves the peculiar nuances of the wellness trade. My wife decided to stay with them, disagreeing, as before, with the way I did business and with my actions. But when I look back with honesty I can say that I was, at the very least, the provider for the safety and health of many.

The Packer organization did have some understanding of how Jurlique products, wellness culture, and natural health all fitted together. And while the executives were busy reading economic magazines and financial records, and exchanging staff, I was thinking about a new level of life and a more relaxed business using the experience I had gained. Eventually I decided that I could no longer contribute to their way of business and they seemed to feel the same way. It's not in my nature to watch with pain and to sit around for long, doing nothing with my skills. I decided that the best thing I could do was to remove myself, and let Jurlique's destiny unfold along on its new path.

But before I left, James agreed that we should have one last meeting in Las Vegas during a big Jurlique event. I met with him, along with his two billionaire friends—new partners in Jurlique—to sort out loose ends of the acquisition and my final exit. I immediately agreed to meet. I had visited the USA many times as it was the country where Jurlique first went global. During the meeting, we mutually decided that it was in the best interests of all parties that I severed my involvement totally. With the business situation fully resolved, I set my sights on living in a country of my dreams, with huge expanses of warm and clean oceans and an ideal climate throughout the year.

I was fortunate to have befriended a former surfer named Darrell who built artistic furniture for Jurlique. He convinced me that Hawaii, a place he knew well, was the right place for me to live and work. I asked him to go there to select a few houses close to the beach for me to inspect later. The first bit of valuable information I received from Darryl was that, on Oahu Island, you couldn't buy a shed close to a beach for just under one million U.S. dollars. After looking over some of the properties for sale, I eventually settled on a white two-story villa on the famous windward side of Kailua. The asking price was horrendous, but was finally reduced by $2 million. At the time of the purchase, my new love, Karin, was in Switzerland. We arranged to meet in Bangkok before flying together to inspect the house, which we both agreed was the perfect match for a new beginning. It was ideally located forty feet from the turquoise Pacific Ocean and was surrounded by a host of celebrity neighbors, including Michelle Pfeiffer.

But while the Kailua property was in many ways the perfect place, Karin and I were swept away by the famous and, at that time, very affordable Sullivan Estate on the North Shore of Oahu. The famous Estate is not far away from Pipeline Surf Beach, where the waves rise to sixty feet during the world's biggest surf tournament in the month of November. Sullivan Estate is perched on a hilltop with superb ocean views; the roar of the surf and the humpback whales can be seen and heard from November through to February. This became our dream home and future work place for about five months of each year.

The real appeal of the Estate, and the main reason why we purchased it, was that the property could be easily developed, with little cost and the right design, into something better. Karin, skilled as an interior designer, manager, and administrator, was thrilled to build a luxury wellness spa inside the Estate where I could build the prototypes of my new ideas and inventions. She set about adding a yoga sala, a meditation pavilion, a health and fitness center, saunas, beauty and massage rooms, as well as hydrotherapy and the launch of my new invention, the JK7-Spa Sensator. In the meantime, I built my own alchemic laboratory for the development of new health and skin products that would set the tone for nutraceuticals and advances in wellness.

After Christmas 2004, I invited my four children to Hawaii to see my new life firsthand, and to get to know Karin. At first they seemed apprehensive, but after a while they warmed to the fact my life change was not only inevitable, but also the best direction for everyone. Deep down, I knew that the transition from years of active involvement to a period of semiretirement, even with a more active spiritual and creative life, would never be easy.

The agreement I had with the new Jurlique owners stipulated that I withdraw from being involved with any organically based skin care products for a five-year period. I was determined that I would enjoy this time as a period of freedom, and see it as an open window for new creativity, rather than as some kind of penalty. While I welcomed a quiet change from the fast lane, as I approached my sixtieth year on earth, I somehow could sense that my journey of discovery was far from over. It seemed life still had more exciting secrets to unveil.

CHAPTER 15

THE CRYSTAL MOUNTAIN

An alchemist is taught how to use the threefold process of separation, cleansing, and reuniting. I wanted to go one step further and perform alchemy on my own being by first cleaning up the body and mind and then liberating the metaphysical state from the inside out.

I figured that if it were possible to go to the next level of awareness, then to do so would require breaking away from the residual energy that mires and burdens all of us conditioned human beings. But was it possible to unshackle the rigidity of past evaluations, invalidations, and judgments that pile up in the mind, overloading and smothering mental and sensory perceptions?

My own observations of life as a health practitioner, businessman, and alchemist were that what prevents people from taking the decisive journey—from the known into the unknown—were their commitments and distractions of work, family, and material possessions. Most humans spend their lives cocooned within a restricted, repetitive, mundane, and compulsive lifestyle, obsessed with these three and other considerations. And those very few who can break free from the magnet of life's conditioned states are still vulnerable to incessant judgments and prejudices based on material values and fear. It is rare to find an individual who isn't trapped inside his or her own self-imposed belief system. Few people, it seems, have the willingness and courage to strip down to their bare essence of existence, based on past experience, and engage with the nakedness of pure reality, which is the ultimate truth in the now.

The temptation to drift in life can be overwhelming, and unfortunately it results in a wasted opportunity to raise the standard of human existence in the process of growing oneself and contributing to others and the planet. Most people live their lives forever seeking a better and more elaborate comfort zone—always wearing rose-colored glasses without any desire to change the lenses. Their picture of their lives, which is based in the past, will therefore be largely the same as it always was.

I felt more than a little uneasy settling into "easy street" after buying a dream house in Hawaii with my soul mate Karin. The cause of a still existing residue of discomfort could not be explained in rational terms as, on the surface, life had indeed delivered much more than I could have ever possibly imagined. Yet, as much as I relaxed and tried to enjoy every new moment of time, there was a nagging awareness that something more was about to be unearthed. As the sunny days in paradise wandered by, this awareness of uncertainty grew stronger. I was itching to contribute and make a difference in a new way, and to not only be comfortable in myself.

When one cycle in life ends, and the patterns for a new beginning start to emerge and take shape, it is time for an alchemist to clean up all the possibilities that started to pile up before the gelling stage. What I had learned from experience was that the Tao of life was the essential energy for the existence and fusion of the human body, mind, and spirit. The Tao is the interdependent force of all attraction—the godliness in us that envelops the heart and rockets the mind into new dimensions of understanding, provided we allow it in. This is the one great secret force that underlies all existence.

I had studied all the main threads of truth from some of the finest spiritual masters who had come to earth in the twentieth century, some of whom I was privileged to meet in person. But all communicated knowledge comes with the provision that truth without experience and personal integration always remains frustratingly hollow. To find truth with substance, a person has to step away from their "Gods in life"—the houses, the kids, and even the precious lovers—to find the true godliness that resides within every living cell of one interdependent lifetime. Then this true knowledge may be applied in everyday life.

Finally, the ideas of finding enlightenment in some lonely

monastery were over. All I had ever wanted was the inner truth and the freedom to be able to apply and live with this truth as a positive contribution to humanity. I wanted the Mahayana heavenly realms without any church. After years of striving, my heart was now demanding one final total engagement with a higher knowledge while, at the same time, my thinking mind did what it had been trained to do best—it delivered moment by moment, down-to-earth solutions for staying alive in the present. My daily routine of inner work and physical exercise kept me going in a healthy state so that I could stay focused on what had to be done.

In thirty-six years I had made and saved millions of dollars and employed thousands of people. I had owned real estate, supported my now ex-wife, skillfully raised four grown up children and had finally found my true love and soul mate in Karin. I knew that if I could just relax with what I had, as the fairytale goes, I could live happily ever after. Alas, life is never that simple and straightforward. Although at the time I was totally unaware of it, a life-changing event was looming on the horizon. Soon I would be given the choice to accept and touch a higher truth, or continue to drift along with the flame of uncertainty while living in more comfort.

Little did I know then that the way to the epicenter of the next level of understanding could only be sought by living on the razor's edge. Something else, which was still missing, would have to come. Inside my mind I knew that something very important was going on. I did not know yet what this would be, but somehow I felt knew that it was approaching quickly.

I returned to Australia in the second quarter of 2004, determined to prepare for a final exit from the lucky country. I needed to pick up a few personal things (that was the logical purpose of my visit), and prepare for a quiet exit. I was still under a lot of pain and hardship with my family. The energies of attraction were already in the mix, and the catalyst was a chance meeting with the novelist, journalist, seeker, and spiritual messenger Claire Scobie, who had visited Tibet on several occasions. I had found Claire to be an intelligent, free thinker and a beautiful young woman, who was one of the few people able to read the percolations of the minds of people around her.

At the time, Claire had recently interviewed Eckhart Tolle in Vancouver about his modern and prophetic book, and instant bestseller, *The Power of Now*. The first thing she did when our paths crossed in South Australia was to seek me out for an interview as the Jurlique Visionary and Alchemist. Eventually we decided not to proceed with the interview and instead had an informal chat about our life experiences and spiritual developments. "You will like reading this," she said to me with an enthusiastic sense of certainty.

Many journalists had interviewed me in the past on various wellness topics while I was leading Jurlique's foray into the global marketplace. Claire was an expatriate from England who commanded a warriorlike attitude toward ethical journalism. A gifted writer, Claire always wrote with a pure heart and only about issues she believed were genuinely important. She was deeply passionate about Tibet.

"Another article," I said to Claire somewhat dispassionately.

"Yes," she replied. "But you'll enjoy this as it shows that Tolle takes the now to a new dimension of understanding."

I looked at Claire's clear, shining eyes and didn't want to deflate her sincerity. " Okay," I replied, accepting her published interview as her personal gift.

As I glanced through the article, Claire explained that she would soon travel again to Tibet. I listened as she spoke about the troubles in Tibet—an ancient culture was on the verge of vanishing from the face of the earth because of China's "integration policy." I was about to leave her, when suddenly Claire's passions for Tibet became more heightened as she spoke about a sacred crystal mountain, Mount Kailash. She paused, and then inquired what I planned to do next.

I was a little startled by her directness and told her that I intended to do something memorable for my sixtieth birthday. Pressed as to why, I related somewhat reservedly that I was seeking a fundamental shift in my life. At that point, Claire took the cue and gave me a full rundown of how Lhasa's population of four hundred thousand was now dominated by more than a million "imported" Chinese, and how the capital city of Lhasa remained the gravitational center for over 80 percent of the Tibetan ethnic group. Lhasa, she said, maintained its status as the cultural center for Tibet despite the mass exodus of many Buddhist monks, lay people, and the Dalai Lama.

As Claire spoke, I took a glance at our surroundings and

realized that were talking together in Adelaide—known as Australia's "church city." It was April, and we could both feel the first winter winds blowing in from the Great Australian Bight, all the way from Antarctica. Tibet, I thought, would be much colder.

I didn't know why I wanted to go to Tibet now. Was it that it was so high and so far away? There was no logical reason, other than it just seemed like the right place to visit at the right time, considering my personal situation on the brink of a new life. In the past I had studied Tibetan Buddhism and had followed the destiny of the Dalai Lama. Claire said that she was on a mission with her friend Kats from England to do kora practice, or circumambulation, around Mount Kailash. She was hoping to find her friend, a Tibetan nun named Ani who was on the run from the ever-present Chinese police.

Without thinking, I asked, "Why don't you invite me and I can contribute to help finance the trip?"

Although slightly surprised, Claire said, "We still have space for one person—another one just cancelled."

She knew that the mystique of Tibet had lured many searchers for the truth. I told Claire that I had always acquired knowledge outside the constraints of materialistic and collective values, and she reassured me that there could be no better birthday gift than going to Tibet. Better still, Claire said she would be delighted if I could go with her friends on a journey to see the crystal face of Mount Kailash—one of the most remarkable and venerated places on earth. The sacred mountain is a holy meeting point for all religions and spiritual seekers, tucked away as it is in one of the most remote areas in the world. It was a difficult place to get to and even harder to walk around. Claire was writing a book about her several trips to Tibet and the heartbreaking story of her meetings with Ani. The trip to Mount Kailash was to be the last chapter in her book, entitled *Last Seen in Lhasa*.

As a genuine messenger for truth seekers, Claire related how Mount Kailash was unique in that it had never been climbed by any human being, as it was regarded by all religions as the most sacred place on earth. Those who have seen the mountain and walk around it (kora), do so by walking under heavy duress. It's a thiry-two-mile walk, without protected walkways, in altitudes higher than eighteen thousand feet. But those who make pilgrimage attest to an incredible power that emanates from a crystal wall on the north face of the mountain.

While billions of followers of Buddhism, Jainism, and Hindu faiths regard Kailash as a supremely sacred site, only a few thousand pilgrims take the harsh journey each year from Lhasa to experience the power and beauty of the earth's most famous landmark, located in a remote, far western sector of Tibet. As there are no planes, helicopters, trains or comfortable buses that travel anywhere close to Mount Kailash, pilgrims first gather in Lhasa and collectively hire a truck for the rugged three to five day journey along rough, narrow dirt roads in the high altitude terrain. It is never below twelve thousand feet. Every day between April and September, pilgrims did kora around the sacred mountain. It takes two to three days to walk around the stunning crystal rock faces, carrying tents, food, and water. Yaks and porters can be hired if required.

For those who can afford it, there are four-wheel-drive vehicles for hire. Oxygen bottles can be carried to overcome sickness from breathing in the thin, rarified air. But, as I was soon to find out, there is no real escape from the harsh weather conditions and rugged country. While exposed to the high altitude, there are only variations in the coldness, barely any good food, and very basic shelters along the way.

Pilgrims and adventurers have been visiting Mount Kailash long before the birth of Buddha over twenty-five hundred years ago and long before the Vedic period that began around 10,000 BC. The history of Mount Kailash is filled with cosmological fables and tales that refer to the mountain as the Axis Mundi—the center of the world. Long before the ancient Indians had written the Ramayana for the Hindu dance and imagery, Mount Kailash was rooted into the heart of all Asian people. Remarkably, unlike other great monumental peaks like Mount Everest in Nepal, the man-made Pyramids of Egypt and the sacred, massive Uluru (Ayers Rock) in Central Australia, no one has dared to put a single hand or foot on the Kailash summit. The Hindus had always revered Kailash as the home of Lord Shiva, the destroyer and rebuilder. Legend has it that anyone who gets too close to Shiva on this "holy of the holies" mountain will suffer instant physical decomposition.

Now totally absorbed, I listened intently to Claire as she

spoke about the extraordinary energy of the northern face of Kailash, and about how the Mount attracts ascetics, yogis, tantric masters, high priests, and wandering monks. "To travel to the sacred mountain," Claire pronounced, "was, for many believers, to take the fast track to enlightenment." To walk around Kailash, however, was a difficult task, as it required an arduous thiry-two-mile circumambulation of earth's most sacred peak. Buddhists walk clockwise around the mountain while the Bon adherents, who preceded the Buddhists in Tibet, walk counterclockwise around the crystal slopes.

Claire warned that the high altitude made any journey to Mount Kailash difficult. Only a few Westerners had been able to master the art of "Lung-gom" breathing, which not only cures altitude sickness but also makes walking far less tiring. As Claire spoke, I was overcome with her underlying message that going on this journey to the most sacred natural monument on the planet would provide a once-in-a-lifetime opportunity to experience what Tibetans call the sacrifice of self for the awakening spirit. How could I better celebrate my sixtieth birthday? It was the golden monkey year for me as I had lived through five cycles of twelve years to arrive at my sixtieth birthday. In Eastern philosophy, this is a major marker, a peak and turning point in life, when one can consciously be aware of this important occasion.

While some of the myths surrounding Kailash verge into the realms of fantasy when I took the time to study the geographics of the mountain—its composition and structure—I discovered that the mountain was indeed exquisite and quite extraordinary. Further research revealed that the Mount was also an object of fascination for the great Greek mathematician Pythagoras, who spent twenty-five years studying sacred geometry in Egypt. What astounded Pythagoras was that Kailash's peak is symmetrical with a luminous crystal face that stands spectacularly aloof as a crowning glory with a glacier base and cone of snow. Modern day geologists estimate that Mount Kailash was formed about 50 million years ago, long before the Himalayan mountain ranges evolved into existence about 10 million years ago.

When I told Claire that I would go with her to Tibet, I wasn't sure how I would cope with the high altitudes in a short time frame even in Lhasa, which lies above 11,500 feet. But deep within my being I had a sense that destiny would make this journey a dramatic turning point in my life. I could feel the flame of adventure burning inside of me and I reasoned that a journey to the crystal mountain might unearth more secrets that could finally satisfy my appetite and hunger for wisdom and knowledge on a still deeper, even tangible level.

Once I had decided to go Tibet, all the arrangements quickly fell into place. There was no reason to delay leaving Australia. My children had grown into adulthood, with three of them looking after their own businesses. My ex-wife had been adequately compensated, and the business of Jurlique had begun a new chapter under new management. As my focus moved to Tibet, I could feel all of the bindings in my heart become unshackled. The years I had spent studying alchemy, Taoism, Tibetan culture and Mahayana Buddhism had transformed into the present time. In the early 1980s, I had completed a Tibetan lama course in Austria, and to visit Tibet would complete a learning cycle. Everything I had learned about Mahayana Buddhism was converging into a momentous finale. It seemed that the time had come to vacuum out the old mind and to get rid of all the stored clutter in a remote and spiritually pure, high-altitude location.

Within two days, I had purchased a Himalayan sleeping bag, thick underwear, hiking shoes, a mountain jacket, and a backpack. I bought the best of everything and booked an air ticket from Adelaide to Chengdu in China where I would meet Claire and her friend Kats. From there we would take the short, one hour and fifty minute flight to Lhasa. Within a week of deciding to go to Tibet, I was at the Lhasa airport. Despite a cold, a headache, and some heavy breathing in the high altitude, any weakness in my physical condition was overcome by the mind-set that now, at last, I was ready and willing to reach out and discover what still needed to be understood. This would be the reward for starting a new cycle in my life.

CHAPTER 16

Liberating the Sense Pods

Over recent years, Lhasa, like all other Asian gateways, has witnessed a rapid proliferation of restaurants, pseudo bohemian bars, and Internet cafes that cater mainly to an influx of foreign and wealthy Chinese visitors. I was pleasantly surprised, however, to find that the Tibetan capital—known to indigenous Tibetans as the "sunshine city"—had been able to maintain a predominantly Buddhist culture. Its unique lifestyle was rich with the Mahayana, known as the great vehicle of Buddhism.

Despite the "Foreign/Chinese" invasion and the enforced integration into the greater Chinese collective, Lhasa still maintained an abundance of grand, stunning monuments such as the Jockhang Temple, the epic towers of the Potala Palace, and the distinguished former residence of the Dalai Lama (now a carefully managed tourist attraction). In 2008, the wheel of history was turned back by events in the Uigures region of North Tibet. It was caused by China's rulers' neurotic fear of losing territory. The unsolved Panchen Lama affair is still not forgotten.

Apart from its Buddhist heritage, the other main attraction of Lhasa is the Lhasa River, which flows down from the snow-filled valleys of the nearby Nyainqentanglha Mountains. With an elevation of twelve thousand feet, Lhasa sits in the center of the Tibet Plateau and is the logical starting point for pilgrims en route to the sacred Mount Kailash.

When I flew into Lhasa, the temperature had risen to a cool 46 degrees Fahrenheit. I arrived with a mix of optimism and impatience—an adventurer's zeal. I had great expectations for a life-changing journey of discovery to the fabled crystal mountain. I was eager to keep moving and, due to my unstoppable nature, I unfortunately devoted insufficient time and attention to the primary requirements of arrival. First arrivals in Tibet need to take certain steps to be properly acclimatized to the high altitude. Somewhat naively, I imposed a hard lesson on myself that the body has its limits, and no amount of willpower can overcome the physical limitations of each individual's essential being. I may have been able to swim ten kilometers at sea level, and play tennis for two hours in temperatures over 100 degrees, but at high altitude the mere task of walking was excruciatingly exhausting.

As soon as I arrived in Lhasa I felt heavy and sluggish, a condition that I mistakenly believed could be remedied with positive mental energy and some Chinese herbs. I thought that I should be feeling lighter, and even exhilarated in the higher altitudes, but my condition was the exact opposite. Casting aside all negativity, I checked into a small international hotel on the main road and mentally prepared for the journey ahead. The hustle in the hotel lobby—and the enchanting smiles of the local female porters and staff who welcomed me—all contributed to me steadfastly ignoring all advice to slow down and acclimatize. Instead, I went jogging up and down steep stairs.

After just a few minutes, I could barely walk. My lack of acceptance about high altitude breathing—especially the need to move slowly—affected my physical state so badly that by the time I staggered back to the hotel, the slight cough I had carried from Chengdu to Tibet had developed into a congested cold along with a mind-numbing headache and the early signs of a fever. To make matters worse, an old sinus infection, which had not seriously occurred since my childhood years, suddenly began to manifest in this higher altitude. I reasoned that the travel gods weren't smiling on me, and wanted to give me an extra test, so I decided to rest for the remainder of the day.

My first nights in Lhasa were far from being the ideal way to start a journey. I could not sleep due to difficulties breathing. Had I known that travel offices had oxygen bottles on request, I would have gladly accepted that help. But I was confident that my general condition would improve by the time I was to meet Claire and her friend Kats to discuss the next few days. Colder winter weather with snow was to be expected and the trip to Kailash would not yet happen. It was very late in the season. When I did finally meet up with Claire, her only advice was to stay in Lhasa for a few days to properly acclimatize—she knew the ropes.

Claire's frequent visits to Tibet had given her an insightful understanding of the best ways to cope with the often-harsh climate and the high altitude. But despite Claire's good advice, I decided that despite a lack of strength and what I considered to be a mild dose of short-term altitude sickness, the best remedy would be to keep my body and mind active. I spent two hectic days visiting the popular temples and stupas, included the frenetic Jockhang temple where the remaining lamas and monks participate in an array of activities. What can be seen here is best described, for nonBuddhists, as a Disneyland of religious passion and expression—an incredible display of dedication to a plethora of Buddhist beliefs and customs.

Another unique temple that welcomed visitors was home to about four hundred boisterous monks—who staged what seemed to be a friendly inquisition. Buddhist devotees, sitting on the ground in small groups, wearing tall yellow and red hats were repeatedly questioned about key aspects of their Mahayana faith, including such matters as the nature of the mind and the four noble truths. I also dropped in to see the famous Potala temple, which was disappointing because all of the genuine monks had left. The premises were instead occupied by a group of grim-acting Chinese chauvinists—militaristic officials with no respect for the rich Tibetan heritage or that of any other culture.

I accompanied Claire as she searched for her friend Ani, an "undercover" Buddhist nun. We headed to a famous hot-spring monastery that housed only nuns, and when we couldn't find Ani here, we went looking for her at the local bathhouse. No one seemed to know where Ani was staying, or they were too suspicious to disclose her location, which she had to change on a daily basis. A reliable source finally told us that she often lived in a hut on a nearby, high hill where no Chinese spies would ever go.

After two days keeping up with Claire and Kats as they frantically searched for their missing friend, my physical state began to deteriorate. My increasingly miserable condition was compounded by the fact that I had gotten little sleep due to difficulty breathing. Other symptoms were a viral cold and a nagging sinus headache. Yet despite the discomfort, my spirits were still high. I impatiently reassured Claire that we should begin the journey to Mount Kailash as soon as possible, completely ignoring her concerns that we spend more time acclimatizing.

After a second sleepless night, I joined Claire and Kats to go to a recommended trekking company. After a short bargaining session, we settled on hiring an old Chinese truck and a newer four-wheel-drive Toyota station wagon. We also got tents, basic cooking utensils, and enough food for an eight-day trip. The obligatory travel crew was to accompany us, as well as an observer appointed by the ever-present and controlling government. We were lucky to have with us a very educated and warmhearted teacher and no politically correct controller. We also employed two drivers, two porters, and a cook.

The truck was soon completely filled with three hired passengers, our backpacks, tents, sleeping bags, and the basic essentials for camping and surviving under cold and harsh conditions. The Toyota was filled with the five of us passengers. The trip to Kailash would take four to five days, and we had to rush before the first snow would stop our trip. Even after the first hours on our trip, I knew it would be a difficult and eventful journey.

Our companions drove like madmen along the narrow, dusty, winding, and dangerously primitive roadways. The slow motion of the fifty-year-old truck added to the discomfort, and offered no comfort for my heavy chest cold. My altitude sickness began to crank up to a new level as we crossed over the first of many passes that were higher than sixteen thousand feet.

Time and distance began to slow down and a few short minutes of driving seemed like hours. My pain worsened and my mental energies began to drain. Adding to the discomfort of the altitude sickness was the tension in the car, as Claire feared that her dear friend Ani might have been captured and incarcerated. Every stop along the way became a welcome reprieve from the humps and the loud horns, which, under the conditions, were life saving. Outside, the weather had deteriorated from being bleak and cold into an unhealthy mix of dust pollution and dirty, icy rain.

After twelve long hours we arrived at Shigatse, the thousand-year-old residence of the Panchen Lama. We had traveled only one-hundred miles from Lhasa. The next day we went further to the south, closer to the base camp for the Himalayan mountain range and Mount Everest, and the road to the west was the only route that went all the way to Mount Kailash. This was to be the last major stop in "civilization" before driving onto Saga, our next overnight stop.

As I struggled to breathe, I began to doubt, for the first time since departing from Australia, if I would ever make it to Kailash. My clouded mind questioned why I had subjected myself to such a physically draining ordeal. And yet, despite the hardship, the flame of the quest was still burning brightly. Even while gasping for breath and experiencing hot and cold fever sweats, I still maintained a deep sense of purpose and a resolute belief that something of importance was destined to happen. I was determined to overcome all the pain and to view the suffering as a test that, when overcome, would be a part of the process of self-discovery. My friends were always quick to observe that I was tough when it mattered—physically, psychically, and mentally.

The next day, travel was even worse. The so-called roads traversed muddy riverbeds along the huge Raga Tsangpo River and around the dizzying sixteen-thousand-foot mountain passes. The traffic on both sides of the roads was chaotic. There was really only room enough for one lane of traffic, but that didn't stop daredevil drivers in old trucks from pretending that there were three or more lanes. In my deteriorating state, I witnessed some extraordinary balancing acts over horrendous precipices with no safety fences.

Finally our truck rattled toward the Saga outpost, where a small village restaurant near served Yak meat, sour butter tea, and Tsampa grain, the staple diet for most Tibetans. But I couldn't eat. Feeling totally exhausted, I checked into a so-called lodge, which offered a collapsing, rotting bed and some filthy blankets. Little did I know that the night ahead would be one of the longest and most painful nights of my sixty years on the planet, as well as one of the most enlightening. I did try to hide my condition from Kats and Claire, as I did not want to upset them on their trip they had planned long ago. They both turned in early also, with headaches.

What began as breathing difficulties and a sinus headache led to the extreme condition of sporadic vomiting and diarrhea. The altitude of almost fifteen thousand feet was a few thousand feet higher than Lhasa and added to the rapid deterioration of my health. Never had I felt so fragile and helpless, nor had I experienced such extreme elements. I had tremendous difficulty breathing in the tiniest amount of air as every ounce of my energy rallied to suck in enough oxygen for survival. The driver and the travel company had forgotten oxygen bottles, which are standard to take for foreigners.

Saga is located two hundred miles from Shigatse, our starting point, and so far our journey had taken two days. From Saga it would take another two days to reach Kailash and then, if I could still move, it would take at least another two to three days to walk on a holy kora around the sacred mountains. The final destination of the long journey was nearly as high as twenty thousand feet. But in my state, all thoughts of the journey seemed irrelevant.

My mind switched into survival mode. I was hampered by dreadful headaches, a nonfunctional immune system and terrible trouble breathing even enough air to stay alive. My entire body was rapidly deteriorating as I attended to my now extreme diarrhea and bouts of vomiting. In my life I had endured some severe hardships, but nothing compared to what I was experiencing in these early morning hours, just after midnight in a dirty, cold lodge on the roadside. We did not even have a toilet or running water. Completely exhausted, I was rapidly reaching a critical point. I managed to muster sufficient energy to stagger out of my primitive bed, and momentarily escaped the bug-infested room. I stepped out into a very cold, star-filled night.

Outside in the freezing air at three o'clock in the morning it appeared that somehow gravity had dramatically increased. As I looked up into the heavens, it seemed as if the stars were closing in on earth. Crazy thoughts flashed through my deteriorating mind; I feared that these exceptionally bright lights in the sky might come crashing down on the planet. Such was the extent of my exhaustion that I dared not return to the lodge for more than one hour. I thought that if I did fall asleep, I might never wake up again—or else I would die from hyperventilation and endless coughing. I was too afraid to lie down again.

As I saw it, I had only two options. Either I stayed on and endured more of the same, or I was to head back to Lhasa for proper medical care. I knew that it would take two days of hard driving to get back to Shigatse and Lhasa where I could receive oxygen and medical attention. There was no help in sight—no rescue helicopter or emergency ambulance. My body continued its release of all bodily fluids through vomit and diarrhea.

But just then, when my body was at its weakest, my senses suddenly became razor-sharp. Somehow I became totally detached from all negative thinking, fear, and judgment, and my mind and soul became light—very light—as if I were suddenly removed from my ailing body. Was this the first stage of dying that I had heard about so many times before? Or was this a moment of enlightenment?

As I looked up to the stars which had never before seemed so vast and close, I had the sudden flash of perception that there were as many stars in the universe as there were neurons in the human brain, and just as many subatomic particles in a molecule or an atom. Pondering over the phenomena of numbers and designs, and in spite of my disorientation, I suddenly found my inner being removed from the main frame of my rational senses. In this detached state, I realized quite clearly that while my five senses were now fully alert, they were clogged and mired down by the clutter of past memories, prejudices, and all the psychological garbage I had accumulated from childhood to the present time. I then realized that all thoughts and feelings were just yesterday's perceptions and therefore were no longer real.

In this heightened state of awareness I could see how

the body and mind functioned conditionally. As I continued to gasp for breath, I began to open wide the gates to all my senses. I could see the full light spectrum of the stars, smell the soggy dust in the air, and feel the cold as it ripped through the woolen fibers of my thin tracksuit to my bare skin. Finally, in spite of all the physical sickness, I was able to listen to the absolute silence of the pitch-black night. I felt so lonely, but I was not alone. I felt safe and protected.

At first, such acute sensitivity provided a welcome distraction from my severe physical condition. But even the opening of the senses could not prevent the exhaustion that consumed my entire body and mind. As I stood in the open air, trembling and wobbling around, I could feel myself falling apart from the inside out. If this, I reasoned, was to be my time for death—and the termination of my journey—then it would at least be a welcome escape from suffering. Nothing could compare to this extreme altitude sickness and other symptoms that showed absolutely no mercy as they devoured every vibration of life-giving energy in my body. My spirit seemed to be ridiculed as I grappled with the neurotic pride of whether to give up or give in.

Long seconds became minutes that then felt like hours as time passed. It was now around four o'clock in the morning, and all resistance seemed futile as I looked up to the stars. I questioned what possible reason there could be to risk my life to visit a mountain that now seemed to bear no important relationship to what I believed in and was experiencing. The prolonged sickness had removed all desire to continue with the quest. I could see no sense in making a pilgrimage to any landmark destination. What would be the benefit of traveling further? Had it become clear to me that there was no physical destination necessary for the inner journey of body, mind, and spirit?

But then I had to question what it was that happened to my senses out there in the night. In that deep darkness I sensed the closeness of cosmos and visualized the huge, frightening stars closing in, sparkling as they were with all the colors of the rainbow. It felt like some additional gravity had descended from the sky, but surely the miles of additional rock under my feet were unchanged. There seemed to be a strong force pulling at my whole being. Was there more gravity coming from above? I could hear and listen to the absolute loneliness of the dark night, and I could taste and smell the pristine, icy air. The intense cold penetrated deeper into my body, and yet while I shivered there was something comforting about the cold.

Suddenly, just as before, all pain and fear vanished. I was left with only the thought of how stupid I had been to take sensory perception as something normal and common. In a flash I determined with full awareness that the senses are intelligent antennas enabling the body and mind to receive and respond to the physical, psychological and spiritual environment. But the idea of there being only five senses, separated from each other and reporting to the different quadrants and sectors of the brain, no longer made sense. Surely, there was something more! And if there were more than five senses, then these extra senses must be more than the secondary reactions, or impulse stimulations, that stemmed from the brain.

The crystal-like clarity of my rational mind suggested that I had reached the limits of my sanity, and time appeared to be moving ever more slowly. My thoughts were moving far more rapidly than my sense of time. I then realized that fighting against the force of gravity would be to no avail. The capacity of my lungs seemed to have been reduced to nearly nothing. The only solution I was left with was to let go of all thoughts, all ego, all pain and just STOP. Helen, my last important teacher, had years ago burned the "STOP" sign into my brain and heart. The decision to stop compulsive thoughts, feelings, and mundane life patterns can be a mighty weapon, especially when an irresistible force of the past becomes overpowering. Such an experience of acceptance can put a person on the fast track to the heart of the cosmic force. Not only is this humbling for the mind and spirit, but it can also open and clean out all the "sense pods" that are filled with the stubborn residual memories, feelings, and perceptions of the past, filled with ego and desires.

Yes, now I was ready to surrender to the great force that had shaken up my body and mind like a thunderbolt. As soon as I reached the unassailable limits of my body, the gravitational burden of suffering began to dissipate. By making the decision to stop, I allowed a new reality to enter. The process had brought about a sense of harmony, along with a new-felt sense of connectivity with the cosmos and my true inner self.

Simultaneously, I had released my mind's self-created weight that held onto the past. I began to realize that truth does not travel to any destination or to any mountain, as it is always present everywhere and within.

I saw that any intellectual process is consciously or unconsciously conditioned by the past, and involves the thinker, thoughts, and feelings. True liberation comes when the information of the filled "sense pods" are cleaned and rehabilitated. For the senses to function in an optimal state of being, all the residual junk that has been passively collected over a lifetime has to be dissolved and replaced by a higher level of awareness. Only then can the senses be restored to freely flow again, allowing the mind to have unconditional, pure perceptions. Conversely, stagnation and the long downward spiral of decline occur when our senses, in a symbiotic relationship with the mind, cling to all charged memories. This creates a solidified heaviness, which keeps all memories and feelings captured inside the "sense pods." This is our inherited system for sensory perception, via bioelectric transmission to the brain. The senses begin the process of storing information, which happens mostly automatically in our minds. The senses are the gates to the process of absorbing all thoughts, feelings, and emotional upsets to the point of saturation and neuroticism.

I came to the understanding that my five "sense pods" were filled with the conditioned energy of life's experiences, and that this old energy was contributing to my current misery. Problems occur when the mind refuses to face the past in the present, and instead prefers to project the past experience of fear and pain into the future. The future then keeps on replaying the repeated past, without any improvement in one's quality of life. The conditionality of the mind forces everyone to attach to what he or she has, and this, in turn, creates additional gravitational momentum to keep filling the "sense pods" with more unnecessary garbage.

There can be no release, no liberation nor renewal, until the sense pods are emptied and cleared of the energy patterns formed by one's attachment to past memories. Optimal and healthy living is based on a life of free flowing, unconditional thoughts and feelings, as well as the freedom to realistically choose. When the senses receive and send clear information, the brain, mind, thoughts, and feelings act with effortless, nearly perfect clarity and synchronicity. There is then more balance and harmony, which manifests itself in better health and well-being, no matter how the outside circumstances are.

As I looked up at the astral lights emblazing both the sky and my very being, I felt comforted, humbled, and grateful. I was so fortunate to understand that all living beings are essentially free life forms, always laterally evolving. Humans have the ability to change and transform while traveling along individual journeys. All humans are walking, floating or swimming in the same universal flow of life, collectively. A down-to-earth, old spagyric alchemy process that I learned so well before, can help here: once the cluttered senses are cleansed and filled with pure awareness, there can be a far greater understanding of the primordial, universal source of life. Humanity calls this source by many different names, including Tao, Allah, Buddha, and God.

CHAPTER 17

BLISS WITH SEVEN SENSES

My long night of discovery in Saga, in the high altitude of Tibet, was a totally unexpected climax to a quest that was supposed to end at Mount Kailash. But instead of facing the crystal rock face of a sacred mountain, fate took me to the point of death—an unforgettable experience that broke through all of my sensory barriers to deliver the understanding that all truth lives within, and cannot only be attained through an external quest or accumulated knowledge. What I discovered was that the universal truth lies in the substance of the Now reality and not in the intellectualized, conditioned, and compulsive images of the past.

While suffering almost to death, I was delivered the insight and knowledge that can be known on an intimate level at every moment of one's life. As the early morning sun began to shed its light rays over the icy Tibetan plateau, outshining all other starlight in the fast-changing dawn, I realized that the primary cause of my suffering was the powerful, unnecessary heaviness that pulled my body and all my senses down.

Ancient and recent memories, thoughts and feelings are evaluated by the processes in the brain and then projected by the mind into the future. A kind of fake, illusory present is therefore created by believing that past and future projected thoughts and feelings are real and present. The present, however, is nearly never there. To allow it in, one must have total awareness and courage, complete detachment from the memories and conditioning of the past. Only deep meditation, intuitive lateral thinking, and dangerous situations may temporarily catapult us into the present, which a few moments later again becomes memory and past. My experience in Tibet was extended presence, which I will never forget and never doubt because it was so clear.

I decided to call the whole complex system of senses, sensory perception, receivers, nerve endings, bioelectric connections to the brain, processing in the different brain areas and cells—all of this, as well as the mysterious transformation into thoughts, feelings, and memories—by a new name: the "sense pod." This term has an association with the iPod, and with pods of whales and other animals and complex organisms. These groups should be seen as similar but not the same. As this definition and modern science is currently stating, we have five, seven, or even fourteen different "sense pods" to perceive, memorize, and react to sensual stimuli from our environment.

Our senses are not, however, clusters of material and

residual energy filled with arbitrary attachments that unexpectedly surface from time to time. To the contrary, senses are the governors of our impressions of the world, and the antennas of our bodies and minds. But because of their conditionality, and because of our attachments to the thoughts and feelings that follow what the brain has processed, they become stripped of their free flowing movement and thus their accuracy. In this memorized and saturated state, we cannot understand the communication of the senses as we are holding onto only past memories, pain, and emotional disturbances.

I spent nearly the entire night at Saga totally immersed in the nuances of intense suffering, interrupted by flashes of clarity of awareness. I finally came to understand what the world teacher Krishnamurti said decades ago about the predilection of human beings to build a cage for themselves to restrict their own lives. It took this journey to Tibet to find out, with some degree of certainty, that we are caged inside our sensory system of existence, a system I now refer to as "sense pods." What emanate from the sense pods are all the memories that distort the mind's ability to know the factual truth at any present moment. Humans become prisoners to their sensory attachments, which are inside the many different and often not coordinated sense pods. Charged memories and accumulated residual energy are stored in the pods with little chance of change or liberation, as long as the pods remain saturated with the past.

In my battle against extreme altitude sickness, it was a shock to realize that I might not be able to survive. My willpower and strength of mind, learned from past experience, had been stretched to their limits. All I finally wanted was to give in and let go, and at the same time let go of my fear, anger, and all my neurotic and destructive treats. It was the ultimate act of surrender, which lifted the suffering and gravity from my body and cleared my deeper senses. I know now that while survival instincts still have relevance for human evolution in the twenty-first century, the wise person of today knows when to stop and let go. There is a universal force to which one must surrender if he/she wants to progress, which is far more powerful and wise than any learned behavior on a personal or ego level.

I did not sleep at all during that painful and enlightening night in Saga. At six in the morning I went to Claire and Kats' Spartan dormitory, and told them truthfully that my health had deteriorated, and that if I were to continue without oxygen, I might die. I said I had to return quickly to Lhasa and then down to the lower altitude at Chengdu. They wanted to stop their journey also, but I insisted and begged that they continue. I said I was happy to take the old truck back but they were adamant that I take the Toyota. These two determined women eventually completed their strenuous kora around Mount Kailash. Claire went back to Australia and completed her book, *Last Seen in Tibet*.

I had come through my search for truth thoroughly, and knew that returning to the comfort zone of Lhasa and

Chengdu was not a defeat. My ego and my neurotic pride should have been tormented for not having achieved the final goal of reaching Mount Kailash. It was uncharacteristic for me to not reach my stated goal. But the truth is that I had received more than I could ever have hoped for. I had been able to discover how all human senses function, and got a deeper understanding and insight about the meaning of psychosomatic causes. The crucial decision to stop was the correct choice, made by free will, and was to be rewarded somehow. I said goodbye to Claire and Kats, and let them take the old truck and all the equipment to drive within sight of Mount Kailash. I took the four-wheel-drive journey with one driver back to Lhasa. The headaches, bouts of fever, and dizziness had still not subsided, but my reconditioned senses relished the new freedom to operate without the mind's gravitational pull of the past. I was physically sick but felt as though I was newly born, filled with joy, bliss, and gratitude.

After two rough days of fast driving back, through Shingatse to Lhasa, I immediately checked into a more comfortable room. It didn't take any medical advice to know that I needed to rest. The relative luxury of a clean room and a warm bed presented an ideal opportunity for me to contemplate the truth that had been unearthed in that high altitude twilight zone. I reached for a pen and wrote down the five ways to become liberated from mental attachments. This knowledge has since formed the basis for a new wellness and longevity modality.

1. Let go of the past and all conditioned memories of the senses and projections of the mind, which removes the illusion of the past into the present time.
2. Cleanse and free the senses and mind of false images and fears, by emptying the saturated and overflowing sense pods.
3. Enjoy optimum living each minute in present, without the mind holding onto the past by creating extra gravity physically and psychologically.
4. Allow natural, free flowing access for fresh sensory perception uncensored by a past conditioned mind.
5. Bury the past and engage the now.

I knew that this essence of bliss gained under duress would be important in my future as a teacher, writer, and inventor, as well as in my future relations.

Examining the sense pods, I could now see how each of them contributed individually and collectively to the wisdom and experience of human perception and communication. They allowed one to interact with both the known and the unknown, as well as providing the background of understanding for a greater truth that is greater than what can be known through the intellect.

I further noted that the primary purpose of the "sight pod" was to perceive color and form as one language of nature, memorized as images and later compared and contrasted with new images. No sense is more dominant in our time or so apt to err. By first emptying and then reconditioning the sight pod with the light and colors of free flowing vision, the eyes can be empowered to read the messages of nature through the full spectrum of light, with each color being part of a universal alphabet. The light from the sun and the stars and other chemical and physical processes can be used to guide the mind to unconditional liberation and optimum freedom. This can be achieved in this one short lifetime.

The "ear pod" was made to hear not only harmonious sounds and bad noise but also stillness in nature and our quiet inner life as a creative void. The sound pod system, once cleared of the clutter, can be a valuable conduit to harmonize the healthy vibrations of the mind. Sound can then have the creative power to sculpt a subtle energy pattern from the inside, and create a true perception of outer physical stimuli. Over eons of time, Tibetans have mastered the art of using sound to create harmonic vibrations that penetrate deep into the mind and heart, and alter the patterns of thoughts and feelings.

The "touch pod" was made to keep "in touch" with the sensations of the environment and its reality. Cleaning up the touch pod improves the health and appearance of the skin, as well as other organs that give bodies form and tenderness. No one can escape touch. What a person touches is what he or she also feels psychologically. This is because humans are naturally touch-feel-sensitive beings. A clean and clear touch pod is one of nature's greatest gifts and allows us to "feel reality."

The "taste pod" exists to know and taste life without conditioned, learned judgments. Humans are often driven by their taste pods and food. Physical and mental perceptions are toned by what a person eats and drinks. The trouble is that humanity as a species is obsessed and helplessly seduced by taste. When the taste pod is cluttered by junk-food addictions, life becomes an endless buffet of illusion. This results in sickness, emotional fallout, obesity, addiction, and early death. A clean taste pod puts food into the field of choice rather than into the field of insatiable desire (one need only see the movie *Supersize Me* to be convinced of this). The truth is that a healthy mind has a healthy sense of taste, and then what is eaten creates a healthier body and mind. It is true to a certain extent that "we are what we eat" and less what we think (Descartes was incorrect in his dogma).

The "scent pod" is meant to subtly, but powerfully appreciate reality. As far as order is concerned, scent precedes all taste. If the scent pod is tarnished, then the taste pod will also be affected. Scent precedes all sensory perceptions and is the most subliminal dominator of all the five senses. If there is no scent, then there is no sense for life. The sense of smell relates in evolution to the limbic brain, which we have in common with reptiles.

As I examined the nature of the five senses, while discriminating alchemically and spagyrically all the different components, I realized that there is a powerful sixth pod that was overlooked. This is the sense of gravity. Without gravity, nothing in nature would be able to hold together. Without gravity, nothing would be grounded and everything would float away like an astronaut in space. This, my perception from my unique night in Tibet, would give me the final idea for my new invention to treat and help overcome and transform stress, depression, and psychosomatic imbalances into positive energy.

The problem with the barely understood "gravity pod" is that its effect on the human condition is excessive. It asserts a position of total domination, influencing the brain, the body, the mind, and all of the other senses. The only balance for the force of gravity is the technique of floating in dense saltwater, and becoming at once like an astronaut outside earth's gravitational field. A similar state may be reachable by deep meditation and yoga sessions, but this is extremely difficult with our active minds. Floating in saltwater (ideally in conjunction with meditation and yoga) can allow the sense of gravity on all levels of being to be overcome. Science knows the importance of gravity for being grounded on earth, but there is little understanding of how gravity affects the body, mind, and senses.

After two days of rest I had recovered enough stamina to take a short flight to Bangkok. There, at sea level, my breathing could finally be restored to normal. I met with Karin just in time for my golden monkey birthday. We stayed in the five-star Banyan Tree Hotel for a week's recovery, taking full advantage of spa treatments. Time spent in Banyan bliss gave me the joy and freedom to both relive and further explore the exciting sense pods, the result of my first painful and then enlightening experience in Tibet.

Was there another sense pod beyond gravity and the other five primary senses? If there was another pod, then it had to exist outside of gravity and beyond all other known sensory conditioning.

In considering the waxing and waning between the two poles of bare survival and great bliss, it became clear to me that the seventh sense pod manifests only once all the six pods are cleared and become conscious. With the pods freed of all binding residual perceptions and energies from the past, a person is naturally transformed from being just a conditioned player into a free flowing conductor of perception and life. In such a state of near perfection on earth, completely removed from all conditional influences, there is the freedom to live without any residual fear or images of the past.

This is the awareness and joy of living with and using the "seventh sense": the collective governor, conductor, balancer, and harmonizer of all the other six senses I described. Who is this conductor really? We take it for granted, and science wishes us to believe that the functioning of all complex sense and sense perception happens by chance. But this is incredibly unrealistic. People call the coordinator or conductor by many different names, including the Ego, Self, Being, Toa, and God. I call it here the "seventh sense" and the system for it the "seventh sense pod."

Was there a fast track to clear the senses and enjoy such freedom, at least temporarily, without a long and arduous journey to get there? What if I were able to build a Sensator for the seven senses? This antigravity device would use a light, scent, taste, feel, and sound system to arouse and release the mind's thoughts, feelings, and conditioned by memories of the past. At the same time it would cleanse out all the old junk from the six sense pods. The treatment would be immensely pleasurable and would provide a fully enlightening engagement with all seven senses that has never been experienced before.

The Seven Sense JK7-Spa Sensator could help people in stressful urban environments by giving them fast, enjoyable access to new creative worlds of unconditioned thoughts and feelings, as well as an easy tool to reach states of meditation faster and repair damages of the past. How would they be able to realize the change they desired for so long? They would see the reduction in negative feelings that they had carried destructively for years, and they would notice how much better they could handle stress in business, finance, and relationships. The Sensator provides a truly reversed psychosomatic experience. All the bad, which we received unconsciously via sense perception and the seventh sense pod, would be reversed, better structured and put in good functional order. This would also be felt in better health and well-being and a conscious step toward better longevity, which means to live not only a longer, but also a more fit, fun, joyful, and healthier life.

Karin and I set our minds to the task of building a high tech, but easy to use, JK7-Sensator as part of our stunning spa facilities at the Sullivan Estate in Hawaii. Together, we embraced the challenge of working out the logistical specifications of creating a nongravitational flotation area and a seven sense stimulator in a larger room—not as a claustrophobic tank. This system would be complete with color therapy, body showers of pure essential oils, sound therapy, and meditation designed to stimulate, relax, and clear the sense pods from the past and create new pure and true perceptions for all senses. Suddenly, one is without the daily and permanent overload we are so used to, from our first breath to death.

I had reached the final point of knowing that nature was always ready to unearth her secrets. And she does it always to those who are ready! The only remaining question to be answered was whether humanity was ready to take the next healthy step forward toward new wellness and longevity. Are you ready?

CHAPTER 18

From Survival to Wellness and Longevity: A Global View

Throughout my whole life, from my early childhood onward, I have focused my energy on better health and wellness through nature. My early childhood memories after the Second World War were filled with pain, sorrow, malnutrition, early tooth decay, and endless feverish infections. Joy and health were exceptions rarely found in my family and in the families of others. After my fourteenth birthday, I made a decision to live differently and to help others achieve more health and joy. My grandfather was my first role model—a natural healer—and my early experiences with alchemy and science formed my initial vision for a better life.

It has always been the dream and deep intention of alchemists, magicians, sorcerers, prophets, rulers, and the wealthy to make gold from cheap metals. They have also wished to become immortal and extend their lives far beyond the average dying age of men. During the last few hundred years, dying at an age of thirty to fifty years old was seen as normal, but now we are expecting to reach ages of seventy to eighty. We could get even older—reaching ages of eighty to one hundred twenty and living comfortably and healthily at the same time. Through better hygienic conditions, ample food and water, less war and destruction, and conventional medicine, people in first-world countries are getting older and older, and now have the potential to reach over one hundred years of age.

But there is a substantial downside and a built-in mechanism to reduce this now biologically feasible target. In "good and too good times," we as humans seem to transfer sorrow and suffering from the outside (wars, hunger, famine, epidemics, violence, natural catastrophes) to inner, more subtle psychological and mental areas. This psychosomatic mechanism can lead to the same physical result of an early death. Only fifty years ago, obesity, psychological stress, neurotic pride, greed, envy, cancer, and heart disease were much less known. In those times of war, poverty, and other daily threats, these ailments were not seen as relevant. Now they are acknowledged as real and must be deliberately suppressed by ever-present fear, worry, and ignorance. This is leading to a new generation of geriatric ailments and sicknesses caused by the widespread psychological problems in our modern "civilization."

We as taxpayers pay enormous sums to help lessen the avalanche of failing health in our "fat society." Problems caused by the so-called good life are ever increasing as obesity continues to rise, along with chronic problems of the heart, coronary system, blood vessels, liver, lungs, kidneys, and all kinds of cancers. Our poisoned environment does not help—from the still accepted practice of smoking, to polluted air, water, and soil, to combustion motor and power plant fumes, and a shameless chemical and fertilizer industry.

In essence, we are getting older. The price being paid for living longer lives is that we are so sick—full of misery and fear of death—that we cannot enjoy the gift of living longer than our ancestors lived. Our lives are superficially held together and barely maintained, fueled by an ever-greedy profit lust and the avarice of the global medical and pharmaceutical systems. They work hand in hand with political majorities and lobbies, which "democratically" rob the taxpayer of their money and health. It is misleading and simply false to call these people health ministers and health departments; the right names would be "ministers for sickness and disease" and "sickness departments."

What a costly "health" system, a system that cultivates misery and hopelessness! Is it really worth it to get older? We are kept barely alive, numbed by pharmaceutical chemicals with incredible negative side effects and with no healing ability at all. Medical lobbies and scientists who believe themselves to be omniscient sabotage us. Where are the joy, bliss, and fun in our lives?

There is only one way out of this misery. With common sense, which is lacking more than ever, one could pursue a much cheaper, pain-free, and joyful way—a natural pathway based on the knowledge of the last three thousand years. Nature's secrets are unearthed in the caring hands of real healers. Their committed supporters would quickly replace a worn-out sickness system that only treats symptoms and therefore keeps diseases going. By a caring and much cheaper approach that is based on prevention, we could maintain good health and wellness. This would keep us fit and healthy—physically, mentally, psychologically, and sexually—into the high age of ninety to one hundred and ten years. In one word, this would be *longevity* put into practice. Longevity for people makes natural sense when we change globalized poverty and pollution at the same time. This unfortunate system has mostly helped to make the billionaires richer and the poor poorer.

Yes—there is a way, now and in the future, for the human race not only to survive longer on this ailing planet but also to live with more joy, fun, positivity, and creativity. Coming generations do not have to repeat the cycle of suffering that is marked by destruction, early death, sickness, and only intermittent periods of rebuilding. Sadly, it is the enormous starvation and poverty in second and third world countries that permit the other half to live the so-called good life, which is not good at all. In fact, it is a runaway train to self-destruction.

Even current, better, "greener" intentions of people to save the planet seem to be, when looked at closely, misused to capitalize on taxpayers' fear and make big profits. For instance, is Al Gore really green? What about the huge sums of money he has made in the last ten years? Others should have received a Nobel Prize for trying to save our planet from ruthless exploitation. They started their work in the 1970s and gave their lives to a movement of environmentally conscious people. And they always paid for their activities, never receiving fat attendance fees just to show up like a movie or rock star. As long as alternative energy supply is not in the hands of individuals, it will be globally administered by the old power, car, and war lobbies—and we can be sure it will be very expensive.

Better individual longevity and a global decrease in environmental pollution go hand in hand, and are closely interconnected. The focus on carbon dioxide alone seems to be the biggest lie of our time—it is primarily a very lucrative business for global players who never cared about people or the planet, but only about new profit margins. Visit any of the bigger cities on earth, and you see people choking from bellowing colored chemical clouds consisting of deadly gases like nitric oxide, nitrogen dioxide, sulfur dioxide, and worse. Why not start here, and stop the enormous deforestation at the same time? It is true that we all must put forth effort to save our forests and quickly plant new ones in addition. But while enough trees will solve the carbon dioxide problem, they will not solve the problems caused by these other deadly pollutants.

Longevity (accompanied by good health, physical fitness, and fun) is cheap and feasible with the right education and action. Complementary medicine, which uses the basics of conventional medicine—operations only when necessary, drugs only for serious life-threatening cases, no antibiotics for colds or for kids—combined with the enormous knowledge of nature-based, alternative, healing medicine, is the only answer for better longevity. However, this would cause less return on investment in the medical field and an end to ultrainflated profit margins.

The established mentality of easy money is still fighting against the new health revolution. An army of a million old, sick, helpless people is an incredible business for those old and proven forces. Ever-fewer multinational organizations are controlling the basic "needs" of people on this planet: nutrition, drinking water, medicine, science, cigarettes and narcotic drugs, as well as energy and the research for renewable energies. In the United States alone, every person consumes a yearly average of an unthinkable sixty kilograms of chemical additives—flavor enhancers, MSG, colors, preservatives, and so forth—most of them totally unnecessary! The damage to our livers and other organs is unknown, but will shorten our life span and the life of every cell in our bodies. All of these influences support the opposite of longevity, and make even the lives of wealthy people sicker and shorter.

At least 100 million people are killed yearly—probably more than all wars in human history—by consuming sugar and other carbohydrates like corn syrup, fats, protein, bad animal fat, sweet sodas, and all the other junk food compounds, as well as enormous amounts of tobacco and alcohol. Even Stalin, Mao, Hitler, Pol Pot, Idi Amin, and other dictators, in their enormous cruelty, needed many years to reach such horrendous figures of death.

And did you know that modern medicine, doctors, and pharmaceuticals are killing about two hundred thousand patients yearly in the United States, totally unnecessarily? This little-known section of today's medicine even has a nice name: Iatro Medicine, which means illness and death caused by medical advice! About two hundred thousand deaths in the United States, extrapolated over the world population, totals at least four million dead from mistakes made by medical doctors and their prescribed pharmaceuticals.

Our civilization seems to adapt quickly to bad news and bad habits—why have we permitted ourselves to get used to this level of numbness, ignorance, and stupidity? Is it because we cannot face the pain, worry, and fear caused by such terrifying and troubling facts, which are global and concern us all? We seem to be so busy with our individual lives, filled with small fears and sorrows, that we have lost the bigger picture. Our greed in our day-to-day survival has taken all our attention, and we have thus left it to others to exploit us.

Globalization has brought people on the planet closer together, in both positive and negative ways. Only a holistic approach to longevity can save us all from a global catastrophe wherein all will suffer more than ever before—the rich as well as the poor. Even Nature herself seems to be in tune with our unspoken goal to destroy life on planet earth—quickly and conclusively. Was the experience with humans on earth a failure? "No worries, mate," as we say in Australia. Nature will recover faster without us!

The financial crisis of 2008 were unthinkable even twelve months earlier, and will have a substantial negative influence on global health and general wealth. It has already been seen to have a great impact, mostly on kids in third world countries like India. The big question is, how can the same people who have created this crisis be the top financial and political advisers of the new American president? Shall we be prepared to expect much worse things to come? Common sense would suggest this!

The personal greed and envy in normal people has been potentiated and provoked to a bursting point by groups of power brokers and their willing investment helpers and manipulators, who are not obliged to be responsible and will continue just as before. Everything is built now on brittle hope, which is traditionally the farmed field of churches and other belief systems. The beaten investors, mostly atheists I presume, will not get help from old belief systems as they are also only financially self-interested. Truly, how rich are the wealthy church organizations, and how poor are their servants and followers?

Unfortunately, the peak and destruction of life and values, through money manipulation and so-called structured products, may not have yet been reached. Inflation, deflation, stagflation, depression (physically and physiologically), enormous joblessness, corrupt and delighted political systems taking over yet more control of people and finances from the pockets of tax payers—all of these factors will hopefully not lead to a fast and complete catastrophe for people and the planet in the next few years. But the scary truth is, that may be the case. Madness and confusion will increase dramatically, both in leaders and on the ground, in a classic case of "Shepherds and their Sheep."

We can choose to stay sane, gain more clarity, goodness, and benevolence. But for such a dramatic change to occur, we need a complete renewal and transformation, which I summarize under the expression of *longevity*—collectively and individually.

The next chapter will explain step by step how such an approach to better longevity could become reality without too great an effort in the field of personal health and well-being. Let us present a first step as how to stop confusion, stress, and fear, and advice as to how to stay sane in times of chaos and destruction. We can each gain the clarity to start a personal healing process from the inside out by applying several known nature-based therapeutic methods synergistically with my new invention and innovation: the JK7-Spa Sensator.

CHAPTER 19

LONGEVITY NOW

In my thirty-year-long quest to find the best and most efficient way to "unearth natures secrets" in our modern time, I have always studied naturally based alternative, holistic and conventional medicine, and I have used naturally based substances to treat chronic and acute illnesses and diseases. Over decades, I practiced Naturopathy, Homeopathy, Ayurvedic, and Traditional Chinese Medicine, and many types of herbalism including Western, Eastern, Australian Aboriginal, and North American Indian. Early on, it was clear to me that most health imbalances are caused by one of three main factors, the first being environmental poisons: factories burning oils, wood and coal, bush and forest fires, volcanoes, and combustion motors. The second possible explanation for illnesses is that they are of a psychosomatic origin, and derive from stress, fear, sorrow, guilt, anger, or another destructive emotion. (Seventy percent of patient visits to general practitioners are related to all kinds of stress!)

The third is caused by genetics, accidents, abuse with drugs and narcotics, or lingering personal karma.

The deeper I was able to look, the more obvious it became to me that one should not have the arrogance or the illusion of being able to heal others. It is much better and more truthful to educate others, provide them with knowledge and wisdom, and help others to help themselves.

From a holistic point of view, a limitation is created by putting too much emphasis on the anatomy and physiology of the human body, and by focusing on treating symptoms instead of finding the true causes. One must look deeper to truly heal—otherwise the options are only to repair or replace parts of the body through surgery, or to use drugs that contain toxic chemicals, which always cause unwanted side effects.

New evidence, first published in 2008, showed that in residents of nursing homes in the United States, there are a large number of drug-induced "Parkinsonism" and dementia cases. Incidences of *iatrogenesis*, illnesses or death caused by medical professionals, and *polypharmacy*, complications caused by prescribing too many drugs at once, are also increasingly published.

Concurrently, new medical and scientific publications indicate that new brain cells can be rebuilt by extreme relaxation techniques as found in yoga and meditation. All of these findings were not thinkable in the last few hundred years. The scientific community is finally beginning to recognize and validate the mind-body connection

Consider chemotherapy, which creates so much pain for the desperate cancer patient and rarely works. Often, it even weakens the all-important immune system, kills many healthy cells, and decreases the body's ability to self-heal. Chemotherapy should be used rarely and selectively. There are serious alternatives available in Germany, but not so in the United States. Despite this, Hollywood actors and even a former U.S. president were completely healed from cancers by nonevasive methods without side effects.

For emergency operations where one's survival is at stake, the conventional medicine of today is incredibly impressive, but is still quite inflexible and fixed to rigid, dogmatic belief structures. Conventional medicine is mostly conditioned by global political and scientific power players, omnipotent drug companies, and tax-paid "health systems." It can take more than twenty years for simple new treatment methods, based on common sense, to finally make headway and convince the medical and academic lobbies to change outdated dogmas for the better of patients. One example is the sensible treatment of stomach ulcers (heliobacter pilori) with only a few doses of a weak antibiotic, as opposed to prescribing useless antacid drugs, which never really helped, but made billions of dollars in sales.

Vitamin C is another example, which has been widely reputed as being useless despite its beneficial effects. Linus Pauling, the double Nobel Prize laureate (for Chemistry in 1954 and for Freedom—anti-nuclear weapon proliferation—in 1964). He was right to advise Vitamin C therapy for common colds and heart disease, but was ridiculed and disdained by the medical lobby because he was not a medical doctor and had "only" common sense. Many doctors still sarcastically refer to vitamins and other supplements as "expensive urine." The never-proven lie that too much Vitamin C will create kidney stones is still alive, despite the fact that observed stones were most always comprised of oxolate. The main reason that vitamins have been rejected is that one cannot make big profit margins from nutritional supplements. They cannot be easily patented or financially exploited. We have a huge sickness industry that cannot make any big money from responsible, healthy people who are interested in preventative medicine. Only symptoms of disease are treated, with enormous side effects from powerful drugs. Real healing would mean a dramatic change from pain and suffering to complete health, without symptoms or side effects, as a result of trusting the wisdom of one's body and mind to reinstate balance and heal itself.

Traditional healers can contribute a great deal toward achieving complete health, but are often not given a voice. In and after the Middle Ages, they were hunted and killed, ridiculed, academically paralyzed, and jailed. Unfortunately this was the fate for the "father of modern medicine," Paracelsus, in the sixteenth century. He was hunted for decades by his jealous academic colleagues throughout all of Europe, while learning "on the run" how to heal naturally. Things look a bit more optimistic in our time, as it is becoming increasingly common to fuse the two worlds of Conventional and

Alternative Medicine. These two fields no longer have to be at odds, but can instead supplement each other to form Complementary Medicine.

On a wider basis, however, conventional doctors, the never happy, ever-profit-hungry drug companies and the government controlled "health" systems are still the ruling systems. When alternative treatments and prescriptions *are* used, the patient mostly pays for these from his pocket. Some insurers are compensating now for some treatments such as massage and chiropractic, but it is still a very small percentage. For patients to seek long-term healing instead of becoming permanent drug company customers, they must be able to direct their paid taxes toward the use of alternative treatments as well.

The approval process for new and old herbal medicines is ridiculously expensive and takes a very long time. The same process is used on herbals as is used on chemical drugs, but this process is not suitable for herbal medicines. This is yet another example of the power of the combination of science and politics, of vested interest groups in conjunction with drug companies and bureaucrats. We in the holistic and alternative health community are still often regarded as "quacks," and are allowed to survive only in a precarious small corner—a niche next to a huge lobby—but only so long as we are not posing too much competition. We are forced to "behave," to bare their mockery and their unfair commercial supremacy. "Keep them happy, appear naïve and helpless—even uneducated and unscientific," was the comment of a leading natural herbal company in the 1990s when the European, American, and Australian Federal Drug Agencies and government controllers started to listen to our concerns. They refused, however, to permit health claims for herbal and vitamin supplements, even those produced under the highest standards of pharmaceutical manufacturing and with a long history of desirable benefits.

I simply had had enough, and looked for a modest way of how I could contribute to our time in a different way. This was how I came to found Jurlique in 1985 in South Australia. I knew that a successful, globally active company would have more influence than an individual trained and legally registered as a naturopath practitioner. With the founding of Jurlique I became a pioneer in the environmental consciousness movement, along with a growing group of others who were serious about the newly born field of Wellness.

Today the alternative health, fitness, wellness, and spa businesses make up a multibillion dollar industry, an industry that can no longer be negated. The global powerbrokers have finally acknowledged this truth and now wish to adapt it to their needs—this, after we pioneers had to survive poverty, ridicule, and scientific and political attack. We, the visionaries and innovators, seem to have been accepted, but we now have to fight to stay a leading part of the industry. This new and profitable business is only in existence because we were skilled and able to see the true need of all people to stay sane and healthy in our challenging time of speed, materialism, and growing global difficulty.

As humans we have amassed an incredible mountain of knowledge, practice, and wisdom over the past three thousand years. Professional herbal medicine and supplements are not causing harmful or deadly side effects, but instead have numerous benefits, especially to chronically ill people. Even so, my major question remained, can physically diagnosed symptoms be successfully treated only by physical means?

My studies and experiences with modern psychotherapy, including Eric Berne's Transactional Analysis, O. J. Harris's Script Analysis, Bert Hellinger's family and group-dynamic therapies, and the work of Karen Horney, C. G. Jung, and others, gave me a deeper insight into the roots of mental, psychological and physical imbalances in humans—major causes of chronic sickness and disease. Krishnamurti, Suma Ching Hai, Tibetan Buddhism, Deng Ming-Dao, and Eckhart Tolle all widened my horizons. I have attended psychological workshops worldwide and have practiced all kinds of yoga and meditation exercises. I was still in need, however, of my last wise teacher, Helen Menock, in Adelaide, Australia. She was able to challenge my sick ego states and allow me to face my "pain-body" (as it is called in Eckhart Tolle's *A New Earth*) for a dramatic change of my views of healing others and myself. This has allowed me to see, once and for all, that physical symptoms are not only treatable by physical means.

To begin to heal from the inside out, however, one has to make a conscious decision to shift. As long as we do not stop *now* and drastically change the flow of the old conditioning on all levels of our existence, there will be no shift at all, no balance or harmony, no health (and may I add, no healthy wealth). How do we achieve this realignment of energy? By more years of struggle with our egos and compulsive thoughts and feelings? No. There is a short, sudden, *now* approach that is available to us when we just face consciously and mindfully the big, red, octagonal STOP sign within each of us. Just as we have to stop in traffic in front of this sign for the crucial reason of avoiding an accident, we also can erect our own STOP sign in our mind and say, "STOP. Never again." No more fear, no more wasting our lives with useless, negative, destructive energies like guilt, worry, neurotic pride, greed, envy, lust, gluttony and anger.

Yes, we have the mental power as humans to make a clear-cut decision to become self-aware and stop our self-destruction. With this new awareness, we can face life and find ways to self-treat our ailments and diseases, and prevent early death and a lack of joy in everyday live. My approach to longevity and better health as a contribution to the future was the affirmation: Start *now*! Stop the old conditioning *now*! It is true that "Yes, I Can!" Although Barack Obama's followers have proclaimed the collective, "Yes, we can," it is actually the individual who must come first. We must first start with ourselves to create a widespread cultural impact.

Even while engrossed in making the finest naturally based herbal medicines and cosmetics, I was preparing myself for the next step, knowing the eventual limitations of my field.

I always had in mind that I wanted to contribute a modest solution for treating the number one psychosomatic culprit of our time: stress. Stress causes so many related imbalances and illnesses that are serious, acute and chronic. These illnesses involve heavy consequences: less joy in life, physical, psychological and mental discord, depression, age-related diseases like Parkinson's and Alzheimer's, suicidal thoughts, and early death.

My idea for a new invention, which would confront stress and its physical manifestations head-on, was finally born around 1998 in Queensland, Australia. A leader in the luxury resort and spa industry asked me to invent the next generation of spa and health treatments for his fast-growing industry. He felt it was becoming boring, and that there were endless reproductions of the style of spa and treatments. As a pioneer in the early days of the spa industry, I had observed the same. There were so many greedy, cheap copycats, and freeloaders who wished to become rich quickly and with little work. Everybody wanted a stunning spa facility and new treatments, and the times were much easier financially. Before the spa craze, such people had been involved with every craze before it: fitness gyms, saunas, pools, hydrotherapy, and Vichy treatments, expensive electro driven massage beds for facials and massages, mystery showers, and service menus richer in quantity and more complex in words than those of Chinese or Thai restaurants.

The industry needed a new, exciting injection of freshness and proven natural therapies—not more Spa gadgets. It needed something fun, healing, and at the same time penetrating and sensational. Adrian was right, but I was still so busy with my fast growing company that was, at the time, involved with the 2000 Sydney Olympics. I was also overloaded with family, traveling globally as a public speaker, writing, and forming the necessary plan of exit from my company.

Nevertheless, I kept the suggestion in mind and over the next decade, came to form my new innovation.

I needed a change from linear to lateral. The result was an invention, which came intuitively and was out of the blue—totally unexpected. It consisted of no herbs and supplements for intake, no surgery, no hospital, no fitness center, no pool, and not even a massage-trained spa therapist. But when the first primitive version of the JK-7 Spa Sensator was born in my mind, lots of details were still missing. It took another nine years of drawing, constructing, and optimizing several prototypes until a well functioning innovation for spa-goers and customers was ready in Oahu, Hawaii in 2008. Its patent had been registered, and it was ready to be tested by critical people from all areas of life. I was excited and motivated, but also skeptical. Was I again too far away from the conditioning of people and the now-booming spa industry that was becoming mainstream? Would it again take ten to twenty years for acknowledgement and success to occur, just as with my spa and natural health ideas twenty to thirty years ago? Would I be patient enough and have the drive and motivation to persist? Perhaps there would be a breakthrough in less than five years, as everything seems to move much faster in this time.

I no longer choose to rely on outside success, and do not need to make lots of money. I also made a commitment to myself that I will keep: I pledged to not take any money personally from the sales of the new innovation, and will give all my profits to charity projects in Third World Countries—some of which I have consistently supported from 2000 on. With this as my position, I could now sit back and relax. I needed only to offer advice and support. I felt that the dream I've had for thirty years might just happen differently this time. People, intuitions, and scientists seem to be more open.

I still had a great deal of searching to do: what did I wish to achieve? I was using the knowledge and experience of my past while filling in gaps in my understanding of psychosomatic illnesses and treatments. I learned about the fields of sensory perception, neurology, and stress, as well as the related mental and spiritual faculties. I studied while I built the spa Sensator, and did so without the stress of making and maintaining income. My wife Karin became the perfect missing half to bring it to the market and convince industry stakeholders that they would get a forward thinking, effective innovation. It provided solutions to the existing problems of clients as well as a breath of fresh air for the saturated spa and wellness industry. Karin's gentle and professional people skills for design, education, and sales-oriented marketing were admirable.

While optimizing the invention, I found ample evidence in the scientific and medical fields that I was on the right track. The latest findings of risk takers, pioneers, and some courageous institutions seemed to be miles ahead of their established conservative medical colleagues. Brain research with regard to stress and other psychosomatic conditions such as sleep disorders showed that treatments involving meditation and yoga produced stunning results. These studies are getting increasing scientific and social recognition, and they are in the exact field where my invention, the JK7-Spa Sensator, will and can contribute substantially. And it can do so with the "side effects" of joy, fun, and even entertainment, in conjunction with its more serious healing benefits. No hype; no unmet promises; just results.

To create the finished product, I combined four separate alternative health treatments to create a holistic new whole. These different methods work together to enhance and synergistically create a safe, uncomplicated, nonthreatening, and fun healing environment. The proof is in the pudding, as they say; just ask people for their testimonies after just a forty-five-minute session in the JK7-Sensator. A middle-aged man from Italy said, "No fear, no guilt, zero stress for nearly one hour. I forgot completely my daily worry about finances ... and it seems to last afterward." A middle-aged woman from Tokyo said, "Unsurpassed! I tried drugs for fifteen years, hospitals and holistic medicine to get rid of my ever-present lower back pain. I was painless first time in one hour treatment in the JK-7 Sensator. Even after one week I still feel better." And lastly, an Australian surfer said, "Mates, that was the greatest surf of my life."

What a *now* experience: stress free time for complete relaxation—no fear, no worry, no sorrow. What a great first step toward a stage of deep meditation, which is normally very difficult to achieve (the ever-busy mind is the greatest saboteur). After a session one receives other treatments like professional yoga lessons, meditation, tai chi and qigong classes, counseling, and massages. Now, one is ready to receive and learn, as he or she is in a totally relaxed and physically pain-free state, with a clear and positive mind.

The probability is very high that the JK7-Sensator will be very desired in the psychosomatic healing field in the future. It stretches its treatment and applications from chronic stress to depression (including suicidal tendencies) to the causes of serious chronic illnesses. I believe it is just the right time to help extremely stressed professions such as investors and their victims in the growing global financial crisis. As people suffer the fears of job loss, a shrinking economy, and higher taxes and are caught in a trap of fear and hopelessness with confused minds and strained health, the JK7-Sensator can offer much needed release and rebalancing.

But how does it work? The experience starts by using all the senses in a controlled and structured way to reverse the negative effects and memories we have stored since birth. First we store our sensory experiences physically (brain) and then psychologically (mind), where they manifest as confusion, stress, and mental disorders, and later appear as acute and chronic conditions. No one could make a valid argument against this automatic chain of events that starts with our senses, the windows to our mind, soul, and body. My simple conclusion: Why not use the same process to treat these symptoms, but in reverse?

All the problems we have, come originally by way of our sensory perceptions. These perceptions are carried by the nerves and neurochemicals to the brain, where they are turned into memories. The resulting thoughts and emotions are mostly automatic and compulsive, and cripple us with confusion, fear, worry, guilt, greed, and envy. They are nearly impossible to stop, and it is quite challenging to achieve and maintain deep relaxation as a countertreatment with yoga, meditation, qigong, tai chi, or a similar practice.

The JK7-Sensator allows us to slow down and stop this automatic mind game, which is programmed by endless past impressions and experiences. It is like a cleansing process for too much accumulation of conscious and subconscious material. During the process, one is in a stage of deepest relaxation—like a deep sleep phase at night—but stays awake and aware. At the same time, we offer to all the senses a healthy, easily understandable way of perceiving pure sensual impressions. This lets us relax, let go, and create a refreshing emptiness, which is needed for deeper relaxation and meditation. When we stop the old "thought and feeling machine," we can recover, refill, and reprogram our ailing minds with positive, pure impressions and material. We reorient ourselves toward health and self-healing The negative psychosomatic symptoms and causes are stopped, and the brain and mind are flooded with new, clear, reduced, and uplifting impressions.

Six different applications are used in a forty-five-minute treatment session, each of which relate to the six senses (as discussed previously) and their coordinator and conductor, the seventh sense. The session is divided into seven cycles with six shorter cycles in between. The total sensory system, with its gateways to the brain, memory, and mind, is fully engaged—but with clear and stress-free, easy graspable logical impressions. It is safe, clean, and comfortable.

The natural therapies include color therapy, sound therapy, and aromatherapy, all in conjunction with a feeling of weightlessness in warm Dead Sea salt in a well designed large room (not in a flotation tank). The senses are active and work together during the session: sight, hearing, smell, taste, touch/feeling sensation, and no or low gravity perception. One has a full, strong seven times changing bath for forty-five minutes. While experiencing seven very strong main colors, at the same time, he or she hears seven selected sounds and smells seven pure essential oils; each happens parallel and in sequence. Colors, in the sequence of the rainbow, dictate the order of the other senses and perceptions. One seems to drift slowly into a larger space—a misty and pleasant environment—while one floats without physical weight in warm, highly concentrated Dead Sea saltwater. As a result, untold therapeutic benefits on the mind, body, and psyche unfold.

Is the JK7-Sensator only a material and physical thing,

a machine that we can touch and understand? Is it a lifeless, inanimate object, or a mysterious vibration generator with some technical tricks to impress? Is it just another small add-on and extension for existing spas, hotels, resorts, and adventurous people? Is it not complex enough for our high-tech minds? To all of the above, the answer is no. The personal experience and results induced by the JK7-Sensator are stunning and unexpected—truly a *wow* feeling that lasts. It takes a person back to the basics in a new, more sophisticated context. While the idea behind it is essentially very simple, it is comprised of complex software, is fully automatic and has a touch-screen computer, pumps, mechanical and electronic parts. It is safe, complete, and easy to use as long as one employs common sense and practicality.

We just built a small version for two people in our new home in Switzerland. Would you like to visit and try out the commercial version of it in Hawaii? Just contact and visit us! You may see it very soon in distinct places all over the world.

Epilogue

My journey in life, business, and the field of health and well-being has led me to the invention of the JK7-Spa Sensator. I see this innovation as a first step and an important contribution to the next era of health, which may lead to a new understanding of the meaning of the word longevity. The JK7-Sensator uses methods that build on traditional alternative and complementary treatments. Many more inventions—of mine as well as others—are still yet to come, and they will further characterize this newly dawning era of health and youth at any age!

When the time-tested, naturally based treatments, herbal medicines, and supplements have finally been proven as beneficial, they will no longer be discounted scientifically. The more unbearable the circumstances in the financial and social future will be, the more we must care for our own and others' sanity and balance of body, mind, and psyche. We must still function within physical means, but with more access to and acknowledgment of the spirituality in and around us.

On its own, the conventional medicine of our time will not solve or heal the increasing challenges to health that we all face. Our bodies and minds are being pushed to the limits of sanity under the stress of our self-created problems and those of our global society. Can we begin with ourselves and help each other to stay sane—with clear minds and hearts? Can we reach an improved longevity, with down-to-earth health, harmony, balance, and joy? I believe that, "Yes, we can!"

Let us start now, with ourselves, and watch with amazement and surprise at what will unfold around us.

Literature and Sources

A small selection only, of books and Websites of knowledge and wisdom, which the author has studied and which he treasures.

Dr. J. Klein "The JK-7-Spa Sensator," Trancending Sensory Perception. Revolutionary Technology for Today's Wellness and Tomorrow's Longevity and "Forever Young" www.jkjspawellnes.com , www.sullivanestate.com

Nearly all of the books mentioned below (also when out of print, as used books) are available from www.amazon.com or www.amazon.de.

Mind, Psyche, Spirituality, & Alchemy

Frater Albertus (Dr. Albert Riedel), *Alchemists Handbook*; Weiser books, 1974
E. Berne, *Games People Play*; Penguin Books, 1964
Edward de Bono, *Six Thinking Hats*; MV-NY, 1997
Edward de Bono (by Piers Dudgeon), *Breaking out of the Box*; Headline, 2000
Edward de Bono, *Lateral Thinking*; Penguin, 1996

M. Cheney, *Tesla: Man of Time*; Touchstone, 2001
Dalai Lama, *The Art of Happiness: A Handbook of Living*;
    Riverhood Books, 1989
Suma Ching Hai, *The Key to Immediate Enlightenment*; Taiwan, 1998
T. A. Harris, *I'm OK—You're OK*; Arrow, 1995
Bert Hellinger, *Gottesgedanken*; Koesel, 2004
B. Hellinger, *Acknowledge What Is*; Tucker & Co, 1999
T. Cleary, *The Book of Balance and Harmony: A Taoist Handbook*;
    Shambhala, 2003
T. Cleary, *The Taoist I Ching*; Shambhala, 1986
Karen Horney, *The Neurotic Personality of Our Time*; Norton, 2004
C. G. Jung, *Alchemical Studies*; Princeton University Press, 1983
J. Jungehuelsing, *Ein Jahr in Australien*; Herder Spektrum, 2007
M.M. Junius, *Spagyrics*; Healing Arts Press, 2007
R. Kiyosaki, *Rich Dad Poor Dad*; Warner Books, 2000
J. Krishamurti, *The Book of Life: Daily Meditations with K.*;
    HarperSanFranc.1995
J. Krishnamurti, *You Are the World*; KM Foundation, 1972
J. Krishnamurti, *That Pathless Land*; Chetana PLtd, Bombay, 1983
Helen Menock, Seminar material 2000–2002, Adelaide
Deng Ming-Dao, *365 Tao: Daily Meditation*; Harpers SF, 1992
Deng Ming-Dao, *Chronicles of Tao: A Secret Life of a Tao Master*;
    HarperCollins, 1993
Dr. Werner Nawrocki, *Transformation*; Alpha & Omega, 2003
C. Scobie, *Last Seen in Lhasa*; Rider, 2006
R. Steiner, (J. Barnes, Spiegeler) *Nature's Open Secrets: Introduction to
    Goethe's Scientific Writing*; Anthroposophic Press (USA), 2000
P. G. Stoltz, *Adversity Quotient @ Work*; John Wiley & Sons, 2000
S. Tenberken, *Das siebte Jahr*; Kiepenhauser & Witsch, 2006
S. Tenberken, *My Path Leads to Tibet*; 2007
Eckhart Tolle, *The Power of Now*; Namaste Publ., 2004
Eckhart Tolle, *A New Earth*; Penguin, 2006
J. M. Twenge, *Generation Me*; Free Press/Simon & Schuster, 2000
John E. Warren, *Your Hidden Carrier*, Wakefield Press, South
    Australia, 1993

Senses and Sensory Perception, Psychosomatic Medicine, Health

P. Barach, *Deadly Mistakes that Doctors Make: 100 Most Common Medical Blunders*; Boardroom Inc., 2007

G. Beck, *An Inconvenient Book: Real Solutions to the World's Biggest Problems*; Threshold Editions, 2007

S. Benge, *The Tropical Spa: Asians's Secrets of Health*; Periplus Editions, 2008

H. Boon, *The Complete Natural Medicine Guide*; Robert Rose Inc., 2004

G. Bodecker, M.Cohen, *Understanding the Global Spa Industry* M.; Butterworth-Heinem, 2008

H.B. Braiker, *The Disease to Please*; McGraw-Hill, 2001

Bernhard Burt, *100 Best Spas in the World*; The Globe Pequot Press, 2003

J. Chapman, *Ultimate Spa: Asia's Best Spas and Spa Treatments*; Periplus Editions, 2006

A. Chevallier, *Encyclopedia of Herbal Medicine*; DK, 2000

R. Firshein, *The Neutraceutical Revolution*; Riverhead, 1998J. Goldberger, *Seeing, Hearing, and Smelling the World*; Howard Huge Medical Institute, 1995

M. Haeffner, *Dictionary of Alchemy*; Aquarian, 1994

D. Hoffman, *Medical Herbalism*; Healing Art Press, 1998

D. Hoffman, *Herbal Handbook*; Healing Art Press, 2001

K. Horney, *Our Inner Conflicts*; Norton and Co/Fischer, 1945/1994

K. Horney, *Self-Analysis*; Norton, 1994

M. Hutchinson, *The Book of Floating: Exploring the Private Sea*; Conscious Classics, 2008

M. Hyman, *UltraMind Solution*; Scibner, 2009 2008

W. Kahle, M. Frotscher, *Nervous System and Sensory Organs*; Thiem, 2003

Ch. S.Kilham, *The Five Tibetians*; 1999

M. Konner, *The Trouble with Medicine*; BBC Books Sydney, 1993

P. Love, *Hot Monogamy*; Plume Penguin, 1998

Lipsitt.; *Psycho-Somatic Medicine*; Oxford University Press, 1977

John Kobat-Zinn, *Coming to Your Senses*; Hyperion, 2005

Cora Daniels, "The Man Who Changed Medicine"; *Forbes Magazine*, Nov. 29, 2004

R. Moynihan, *Too Much Medicine?*; ABC Books, 1998

Noah McKay, *Wellness at Warp Speed*;Mandala Publishing, 2008

G. Null, *Power Aging*; Bottomline Books, 2003

N. Goodrick-Clarke; *Paracelsus: Essential Readings Publ.*; 1999

Klavans, *The Medicine of History: From Paracelsus to Freud*; 1982

W. Reich, *The Function of the Orgasm: Discovery of the Orgone*; Condor, 1983

Th. Reik, *Masochism of Modern Man*; Farrar, Strauss and Company, 1949

B. Ross, *Forbidden Cures*; Healthier News, 2007

C. U. M. Smith, *Biology of Sensory Systems*; John Wiley & Sons, 2000

M. Smith, *Health and Wellness Tourism*; E. Linacre House, 2008

M. Stavish, *The Path of Alchemy*; Llewellyn Publ., 2007

C. Steiner, *Emotional Literacy*; Bloomsbury, 1997

C. Steiner, *Scripts People Live*; TB 1980

I.Stewart,V.Joines, TA Today; Lifespace Publishing, 1987

Dr. Theodosaki, *Don't Let Your HMO Kill You*; Routledge, 2000

E. Wagner, *How to Stay out of the Doctor's Office*; Bookman/Griffit Press,

M. Wood, *Vitalism: The History of Herbalism, Homeopathy, and Flower Essences*; N. A. Books, 2000

"How Thinking Can Change the Brain," http://www.dalailama.com/news.112.htm, 29 Jan. 2009

"Der Buddha in uns," www.pm-magazine.de, Jan. 2009

Wege aus dem Stress: wie das Gehirn sich selbst heilen kann, www.spiegel.de, No. 48, 2008

www.healtiernews.com

www.researchmatters.havard.edu

www.spagoer.com

www.spafinder.com

www.asri.net (sleep research)

www.wellnessatwarpspeed.com

www.spasabout.com

www.experienceispa.com

www.earthcharter.com (environment)

www.dailyplanetmedia.com (environment)
www.Jkjspawellness.com
www.sullivanestate.com (first JK7-sensator)

Aromatherapy and Taste

Battagly, *The Complement Guide to Aromatherapy*; Perfect Potion, 1995
R-M. Gattefosse (edited by B. Tisserand), *Aromatherapy*; Saffron Walden, 1993
Max Lake, *Scents and Sensuality, the Essence of Excitement*; Futura, 1991
M. Lavabre, *Aromatherapy Workbook*; Healing Arts Press, 1990
Shirley Price, *Aromatherapy Workbook*; Thorson, Harper, Collins, 1993
W. Sellar, *Directory of Essential Oils*; Saffron Walden, 1992
J. Valnet, *The Practice of Aromatherapy*; 1990

Color Therapy
R. Amber, *Color Therapy*; Aurora Press, 1983
Faber Birren, *Color Psychology and Color Therapy*; Lyle Stuart, 1978
Prof. L. Eberhard; *Heilkraefte der Farben*; Drei Eichen, 1977
Oskar Ganser, *Chromotherapie*; Baumgartner Verlag,Publ., 1975
David Heber, UCLA, *What Color Is Your Diet?*; Regan Books, 2001
H. Irlen, *Reading by the Colors*; Penguin Group, 2002
J. Gage, *Color Meaning*; University of California Press, 1999
C. Klotschke, *Color Medicine*; Light Techn. Publishing, 1993
J. McLeod, *Colours of the Soul*; O Books, 2006
D. L. Mella, *The Language of Color*; Warner Books, 1988
Heinz Schiegel, *Color Therapie*; Bauer, 1979

Sound Therapy

J. E. Behrendt; *The Third Ear*; Element Books, 1988
J. E. Behrendt; *The World Is Sound*; Nada Brahma, Destiny Books; Insel, 1991
Farb Klangtherapie; Energetik Publ.(Verlag), 1972
M. L. Gaynor, *The Healing Power of Sound*; Shambhala, 2000

J. Leeds, *The Power of Sound*; Healing Arts Press, 2001

Philosophy, Religion, Business, Globalization, Environmentalism

Gary Allen, *None Dare to Call It a Conspiracy*; Buccaneer Press, 1971 (see under "Used Books" at www.amazon.com)

G. Allen, *Kissinger, The Secret Side of Secretary of State*; Deven-Adaer Comp., 1979

G. Allen, *Ted Kennedy: In Over His Head*; 76 Press Publishers, 1980

R. E. Allen, *Greek Philosophy from Thales to Aristotle*; The Free Press, NY, 1991

K. Amstrong, *Islam, A Short History*; Random House,2002

Sri Aurobindo, *The Life Devine*; Lotus Press USA, 2000

F. Bailley, *The Fall from Grace: The Untold Story of Michael Milken*; Carol Publ., 1992

P. Ball, *Universe of Stone, A Biography of Chartres*; HarperCollins NY, 2008,

P. Barry, *The Rise and Rise of Kerry Packer*; Uncut, 2007J. Bennet, Gurdjieff, *Making a New World*; Harper Colophon Books, 1973

J. Berg, *The Power of Kabbalah*; 2004

E. de Bono; *Sur/Petition*; HarperCollins, 1992

E. de Bono, J.Lyons, *Marketing Without Money: How 20 Top Australian Entrepreneurs Crack Markets with Their Minds*; Penon Publ., 2003

Bo Yin Ra, *The Book on Happiness*; Kobersche Publ.(Verlag) 1988W. Bonner, *Empire of Debt*; John Wiley & Sons, NY, 2006

W. Bonner, *Financial Reckoning Day, Surviving the Soft Depression of the 21st Century*; Wiley & Sons, NY, 2003

T. Brickhouse, *Plato's Socrates*; Oxford University press, 1996

J. Cutsinger, *Path to Heart: Sufism and the Christian East*; World Wisdom Inc., 2004

A. Diem, *Lions of the Punjab: Introduction to the Sikh Religion*; Kindle Book, 2007

Meister Eckhart, by O. Davies, *Selective Writings*; Penguin Classic, 1991

H. Fischer, *Plaedoyer fuer eine Sanfte Chemie*; C. F. Mueller,

Literature and Sources

M. K. Gandhi, *An Autobiography or Story of My Life, Experiments with Truth*; Beacon Press, 1993
M. E. Gerber, *The E-Myth Revisited*; Harper Business, 2001
Al Gore, *Earth in Balance*; Rodal Books, 2006
B. Greenberg, *King Solomon and the Queen of Sheba*; Pitspopany Press, 1997
Hui Hai (J.Blowfiled), *Zen Teaching of Instantaneous Awakening*; 2006
C. C. Horner, *Global Warming and Environmentalism*; Regnery Publ., 2007
Don Jacobs, *Wisdom and Wealth: 7 Ancient Secrets of King Solomon*; 1998
Jung Chang, J. Haliday, *Mao: The Unknown Story*; Anchor Books, 2006
P. Kahn, *Secret History of the Mongols: The Origin of Chingis Khan*; Cheng Tsui C.; 1998
C. H. Kahn, *Pythagoras and the Pythagoreans*;
Soren Kierkegaard, *The Sickness unto Death*; 1983
S. Kierkegaard, *Fear and Trembling*; Wilder Publications, 2008
R. Kiyosaki, *Cashflow Quadrant*; Warner Books, 2003
R. Kiyosaki, *Prophecy: Why the Biggest Stock Market Crash in History is Still Coming*; WarnerBooks, 2002
N. Klein, *The Shock Therapy, The Rise of Disaster Capitalism*; Pan Books, 2008
K. Knott, Hinduism, *A Very Short Introduction*; Oxford Univ. Press, 2000
P. Kroedel, *Die Kunst des Regierens ohne Politik*; Self Published, 1972
Bhikshu Wai-Tao, *Laotzu's Tao and Wu Wei*; Bibliobazaar, 2007
V. H. Meir, *Lao Tzu: Toa Te Ching*; 1990.
C. Lilly, *The Centre of the Cyclone*; Ronin Publishing, 1972
J. C. Lilly, *The Scientist, A Metaphysical Autobiography*; Ronin Publishing, 1988
J. C. Lilly, T.Robbins, *The Quiet Centre: Isolation and Spirit*; Ronin Publishing Inc., 2003
T. Leary, *High Priest*; Ronen Publishing, 1995
H. B. Maynard, S.E. Mehrents; *The Fourth Wave; Business in the 21st Century*; Berrett-Koehler Publ.,1993
J. Marozzi, *Tamerlane: The Sword of Islam, Conqueror of the World*;

HarperPer., 2004
D. Nicole, *The Age of Tamerlane*; Sprey Publishing, 2003
Osho (Baghwan Sree Raineesh), *The Book of Secrets, Key to Love and Meditation*; Osho International Foundation, 1998
P. D. Ouspensky, *In the Search of the Miracolous*; Arcana, 1988
V. Parikh, *Jainism and the New Spirituality*; Peace Publications Toronto, 2002
A. and B. Pease, *Why Men Don't Listen and Women Cannot Read Maps*; Random House, 2000
J. Perkins, *Confessions of an Economic Hitman*; Penguin Groop, 2004
J. Perkins, *The Secret History of the American Empire*; Penguin Group, 2008
P. Plichta, *Gottes geheime Formel*; L.Mueller D, 1995
J. Priogine, *Order out of Chaos: Man's New Dialogue with Nature*; Shambhala, 1984
E. Radzinsky, Stalin; *The First In-Depth Biography*; Anchor Books, 1997
A.von Retyi, Bilderberger, *Das geheime Zentrum der Macht*, Kopp, 2006
Ch. Riedweg, *Pythogaras: His Life, Teachings, and Influence*; Cornell Univers. Press, 2008
Idris Sha, *The Sufis*; Octagon, 1982
B. Shull, *The Fourth Branch: The Federal Reserve's Unlikely Rise to Power and Influence*; Praeger Publ., 2005
Sklar, *Trilateralism: The Trilateral Commission and Elite Planning for World Management*; South End Press, Toronto, 1999
Rudolf Steiner, *Anthroposophy of Everyday Life: Facing Karma*; Anthr. Press, 1995
Rudolf Steiner: An Introduction to His Life and Works; 2007
Rudolf Steiner, *Goethe's Conception of the World*; Haskell, 1972
T. Izutsu, *Sufism and Taoism*; 1984
S. Suzuki, *Zen Mind, Beginner's Mind*; Shambhala Library, 2006
J. Tauler, *Tauler's Life and Sermons*; Kessinger Publ., 2008
J. Telushkin, *Jewish Literacy*; HarperCollinsNY, 1991
The Tibetan Book of Living and Dying; Harper SanFranc., 1992
J. Toland, *Adolf Hitler: The Definite Biography*; 1991
P. Tompkins, *The Secret Life of Plants*; Harper & Row, 1984
P. Russell, *Upanishads*; Wildwood House, 1978

R.A. Vaugham, *German Mysticism*; HarperCollins NY, 2005
F. Wheen, *Karl Marx: A Life*; W. W. Norton, London, 2001
S. G. Wilson, *Bahaism and Its Claims*; 2008
W. Witherbie, *The Cosmographia of Bernardus Silvstries*; Columbia Univ., 1990